Nora Hopper Chesson

Ballads in Prose

Nora Hopper Chesson

Ballads in Prose

ISBN/EAN: 9783744776301

Printed in Europe, USA, Canada, Australia, Japan

Cover: Foto ©Thomas Meinert / pixelio.de

More available books at **www.hansebooks.com**

DANCE IN YOUR RINGS AGAIN: THE YELLOW WEEDS
YOU USED TO RIDE SO FAR, MOUNT AS OF OLD ♣ ♣
PLAY HIDE & SEEK WITH WINDS AMONG THE REEDS
AND PAY YOUR SCORES AGAIN WITH FAIRY GOLD ♣

CONTENTS.

	PAGE
The King of Ireland's Daughter	3
The Sorrow of Manannan	7
April in Ireland	21
The Three Brigits	25
Silk of the Kine	35
Cuchullin's Belt	39
A Connaught Lament	51
The Lamp of Brighid	55
Ros Geal Dhu	63
Crióch Agus Amen	67
The Wind Among the Reeds	79
Boholaun and I	83
The Fairy Fiddler	91
Daluan	95
Una of the West	107
Soul of Maurice Dwyer	111
Kasár	121
The Gifts of Aodh and Una	125
Lament of the Lay Brother	147
The Four Kings	151
Lament of the Last Leprechaun	163
Aonan-na-Righ	167
Glossary	181

The King of Ireland's Daughter.

The King of Ireland's Daughter.

*Gray sails sailing west over gray water,
Gold rings and gold crown for the King o' Ireland's daughter.*

*Dark rose, dark rose, in the garden blooming,
Break sheath and blow, rose! gray sails are coming.*

*Why in thy long sleep ringest thou, O spear?
Silk we wear instead of steel now gray sails are here.*

*Don your steel and take the spear: lay the silk aside,
Lo! beneath the sails o' gray sits a low-born bride.*

*Dark rose, dark rose, in the garden blowing,
Die, for thou hast bloomed in vain: gray sails are going.*

*Gray sails going east over gray water,
Broken troth, broken heart, for the King o' Ireland's daughter.*

The Sorrow of Manannan.

THE SORROW OF MANANNAN.

THERE were three great sorrows in Eiré once in the days that are buried deep beneath the stones of forgetfulness: and mighty sorrows were these, and men and maidens wept for them: but my tale is of a sorrow older yet, and yet that is not wept for: and its name is the Sorrow of Manannan.
 · They made feast together in the highest hall of Tara: Eterscél, the King, gray with many victories: Conall Collamair, his son: and the Ard Righ of Eiré, who had that day plighted troth to Conall's only daughter, Tuag of the Yellow Hair. There was ringing of harps and tympans, and the sound of a voice singing of old battles, and great deeds done by the King Eterscél, and the High King Feargus, and Conall, their kinsman, and Cu, King of the Clan Colla, who sat at the left hand of Feargus the Ard-Righ, as he might by right of his

name, while all other kings sat removed, the nearest a sword's length from him.

Many songs the minstrel sang: of the men that feasted and the men that slept their sleep: and when Hugh Dall's fingers faltered on the harp-strings, young Colg arose in his place and sang a dream-song that darkened the light of battle in the eyes of his hearers, and paled the flush of battle in their sun-burnt faces. But in the chamber where the Princess sat watching her women comb out the fleece, one maid stopped singing of battles, and holding her silent harp against her breast chanted a whispered song, with her gray-green eyes fixed on her mistress's face. And this was the fashion of her song:

"Sorrow has touched me on the heart,
   And will not let me be:
One woman only stands apart
   From pain that holds the very heart of me:
Yet, Princess, there is borne to-day for thee
A sorrow: and the sorrow of Manannan.

And dost thou go, my Queen, unwooed, to wed?
Or wilt thou rise and follow after me,
   Past graves of women dead,
Whither the Undying Women sail the sea?
Shall gold bespread, or all of amber be
   The bridal-bed for thee?
Thy gift, thy father's wrath? or days that dree
The sorrow and the sorrow of Manannan?"

The skein of shining wool slipped from the lady Tuag's idle fingers, and she stood up slowly, tallest among her maids, and strong and supple of limb as were few women of Eiré. Then the singer also arose from her stool, and she too was beyond the common strength and stature of women, as she stood shoulder to shoulder with the princess.

"Shall we go?" she said.

And Tuag said, "We will go." She looked round the torch-lit chamber as one that takes farewell, and she looked at the waiting women combing their fleece in a dream that kept them deaf and blind. And the woman that had sung of Manannan took up a cloak woven of fine white wool and cast it over Tuag, hiding her long blue gown, and the hood she drew over Tuag's head, crushing the green leaves that were in her fillet; and they went forth hand in hand past kinsfolk that stayed them not, past hounds that heard them not, though their garments brushed their feet. They went through the camp unseen and unheard: past the fences of wattles, beyond byres where the sleeping kine took no heed of them, where the neatherds ceased not from tale-telling at the sound of their soft footsteps. Then they were in the uncleared woodlands, and the Princess clung trembling to her comrade's arm, but only for a moment. For she that upheld her lifted her voice in a wordless song, and sent it pealing into the woods from tree to tree, until it seemed to the Princess that birch and beech and plane cried shame on Conall's daughter for fearing any created thing, and that oak and pine called on her to come, and to come swiftly.

"Let us go," she said: and they walked on under beeches and pines, over last year's leaves and this year's pushing grass, while the bats whirred and cried about them, and the moths woke and brushed their faces with soft ghostly wings.

"I have never walked so fast or so far," said the Princess at last. "Let us tarry and rest: art thou not also footsore, girl, or are thy feet as unwearied as thine arm is strong?"

"Lady, do not rest there—not beneath the quicken. It is an evil resting-place for thy father's daughter."

"How so?" said Tuag, "if I bring a clean heart and clean hands to its shade?"

Then she stopped, and stood dumb in the quicken shade: for the sleep spell was shed now from her eyes, and she saw her companion throw off the woman's robe that now was no disguise, and stand up, a goodly man and gallant, in his tunic of the gentle colour.

"So," she said, in wrath, "it was easy to deceive the woman who took thee in and fed and sheltered thee, because thou saidst thou wast only child of my mother's foster-brother. But here it will be ill for thee to lie—in hearing of the quicken. Give me thy name, that I may know upon whom my father must revenge me. Give me thy name."

"Nay: but I did not lie in all, Tuag. For indeed I am of thy mother's kin, and shortly shall I be knit to thee in even closer kinship, for I am foster-son of the man thou goest to wed to-night."

"Never will I be of closer kin to thee, O false speaker," Tuag said. "Is it Manannan Mac Lir who desires me? Let him take me, then, but from the sea, and not from thy hands, thou liar."

"These be hard words," Manannan's foster-son said, quietly, "Yet will I bring thee safely and with honour to my lord, O Lady of Tara."

"Without my honour thou wouldst bring me only to my grave, O Fer Fi," said the Princess. "Be warned also that I carry a skene in my belt, and what slew Conaire the Black may even drink the blood of a warlock and a princess in one night."

"Thou may'st use thy skene at thy pleasure, daughter of Conall," Fer Fi said, as he drew his own knife from his belt and threw it on the grass at her feet. "And here is mine own, also at thy service, so that I stand unarmed, warlock though thou callest me. And now is it thy pleasure to go back? back to wed with the Ard-Righ? For I put the sleep-spell on thy women, and on the sentinels, and all think thee still in thy chamber. Shall we go back, Mistress? or forward to Manannan?"

"There is no going back for me," Tuag said, with a steady voice. "Dear is Tara, and dear is my shut bower, and dear are Una, and Muirgeis and Sinead that comb the fleece, and Gormshuil that robed me for every feast in my father's father's hall. Dear are the dark eyes of my father, and the gray locks of Eterscél, and dearer are the stones of my mother's grave. And dear are the camp-fires every one, yet I turn nightwards and seawards. Go on, Fer Fi! Manannan has called me, and I cannot help but come, although I see Tara no more."

"The sea is not far hence," Fer Fi answered her, gently. "But there is rough walking to come, for we are at the edge of the wood: and if I may hold thy hand perhaps I may lighten the way for thee." But the Princess shook her head, looking at him with grave eyes, and folded her arms on her breast.

"Go first, Messer," she said, "my help is in myself henceforward." So Fer Fi bowed his head before her, and went first, and as he went he made a song on the rough path that took them seawards.

> "Sharp stones we tread as we descend,
> Sharp stones the tender feet that rend:
> Yet she, my foe, that was my friend,
> Hath sharper words to fling at me,
> As we go downwards to the sea
> All night that called us wearily."

Then the sharp pebbles gave place to larger stones, and these to a little stretch of sand, yellow in the yellow moonlight. And here Fer Fi stopped short, while Tuag dropped down on the sand and dabbled her burning feet in a pool of clear sea-water.

"A little patience, Lady," he said, "and we shall be in the country of the Ever-Living. But we must first find a boat, and round the bend of yon rocks there are huts of fishermen, and there I shall find a boat and oars belike. But will the Princess bide here alone?"

"Why not?" said Tuag. "Have I not here thy knife and mine, Fer Fi? Go hence and do thine errand, and I will wait for thee. None will come to the shore at this hour o' the night—or is it the morn?"

"It is morn, Princess, but the dawn will not come for an hour yet."

So Fer Fi went with long, quick strides across the sand, but he came not back as swiftly. Tuag threw the hood back from her head, and bound up her long yellow hair, and shook from her fillet the withered leaves: then, because the time hung on her hands, she rose up and began dancing, weaving a wild measure on the yellow sand as her mother had taught her long since: and as she danced she sang in a tongue that had been forgotten by all save her mother's kindred, for a hundred years. And as she danced she was aware of eyes and voices and laughter, and a wave broke round her ankles, and another, and another. Then a voice piped in her ear shrilly, "What wouldst have of us now thou'st called us up?" Looking up, she saw a great wave that gathered itself as high as her breast, and there were shapes of sea-children in it: and as it broke against her they clung to her, and cried in their sweet, cold voices, "Thou has called us up with thy dancing, O daughter of the stranger: now what wilt thou have of us?"

"Nothing, O sea-people," Tuag said, and she ceased from dancing, and there was fear in her eyes as the next wave broke on her breast, and she saw herself waist-deep in the sea. Then the sea-children laughed: and one pointed landwards, and cried, laughing, "See, the current that runs betwixt thee and the shore, O stranger: thou hast danced too long and too well, and the waves have come to try who is nimbler and stronger, they or thee." Then Tuag turned her face shorewards, and saw that as she had said before, there was indeed no going back for her. Now the fear of death took her by the throat: and she shrieked to her father and to Eterscél the King. But a sea-child threw his cold arms round her neck, and said, softly, in her ear, "Is it so ill to die then? and if the waves spared Conall's daughter would she live for ever? We have never lived yet: but will not the daughter of the stranger show us how to die?" So Tuag's strength came back as she spoke, and she drew the cold hands to her bosom and kissed the wild eyes and the shining hair. "Keep thy head on my heart, O sea-child," she said "and keep the courage there, while my lips keep their breath." The boy turned and kissed her on the lips, and Tuag folded her arms closer round him; then a wave caught her hood from her head, and all her yellow hair fell down, and the sea-children caught at the long locks and plucked them, and buffeted her face, and beat her hands with stinging seaweeds, and smote her breast and arms with blows that left no mark behind, but burnt like fire. Then the child that lay on her bosom said : " Take no heed, but abide it, thou Fair-Hair. For it is their nature to strike and sting, and it is the nature of the land-folk to abide and die and defy them. And, look, the water is breast-high already : and soon it shall touch thine eyelids, for this is the flood tide." Now there was a little space of silence, and then the sea-folk began their petty torments again, and the water was up to Tuag's throat. And now she felt the child's arms heavy round her neck, and she saw him lift his head from her breast, and she bent down slowly to give him the kiss he asked for. As she stooped the sea-children caught her in their strangling clasp and dragged her down—and down.

Now when dawn came the fishers saw the shine of yellow hair far out to sea, and they put out and brought to shore a drowned woman with amber and pearls twined in her loose hair, and a dead child clasped to her bosom. And as they came ashore with their burden the sea cast up at their feet the body of a man dressed in the gentle colour with a dagger thrust through his heart ; and the hilt of the dagger was of the wonderful green stone whose like is not in the round world, and whereof (they say) Manannan's sword was made ; but there was no wound on the sea-child's body, and him no waves could drown, wherefore the sennachies say that because having seen Tuag he loved her, his life and hers were mingled in death—and in the Tir na n'Og he and she dwell together, mother and child. But Manannan Mac Lir has had no other love and lady; and if you listen any moonlit night you will hear in the sea-music the voice of the sorrow of Manannan.

April in Ireland.

April in Ireland.

*She hath a woven garland all of the sighing sedge,
And all her flowers are snowdrops grown on the winter's edge:
The golden looms of Tir na n' Og wove all the winter through
Her gown of mist and raindrops shot with a cloudy blue.*

*Sunlight she holds in one hand, and rain she scatters after,
And through the rainy twilight we hear her fitful laughter.
She shakes down on her flowers the snows less white than they,
Then quickens with her kisses the folded " knots o' May."*

*She seeks the summer-lover that never shall be hers,
Fain for gold leaves of autumn she passes by the furze,
Though buried gold it hideth: she scorns her sedgy crown,
And pressing blindly sunwards she treads her snowdrops down.*

*Her gifts are all a fardel of wayward smiles and tears,
Yet hope she also holdeth, this daughter of the years—
A hope that blossoms faintly set upon sorrow's edge:
She hath a woven garland all of the sighing sedge.*

The Three Brigits.

THE THREE BRIGITS.

They sat in the uncertain sunshine of a wintry day, the three Brigits: Brigit, the Farmer, old and brown and withered—her daughter, Brigit of the Judgments, a tall and comely woman ripened and sweetened by fifty autumns—and the grand-daughter Brigit, straight and slim as a rush, with all the beauty of her face folded and sleeping still.

Now the eldest Brigit sat nodding in her carved chair, with the sunlight warm on her blind eyes, but the house-mistress, Brigit of the Judgments, sat spinning busily, and her daughter stood in the open air under the blessed thorn, watching her busy mother, with a smile in her dreamy eyes. And as she dreamed, there came a step on the ringing road, and a shadow fell across the girl's feet—the shadow of a tall woman with a face kind and sad and beautiful, who carried a sleeping boy in her arms.

"The gods save all here!" she said, softly, "and bless the work!"

"Come in, and welcome," said Brigit of the Judgments, heartily. Then she raised her eyes to the stranger's face, and her own grew white and strange, as does that face which looks on something that is not of this world.

"Who are you?" she cried.

"My name," said the woman, softly, "is Kathaleen Ny-Houlahan: and his——" looking down with a smile in her grey eyes at the lad in her arms, "Oh, one may call him Aongus (Love), or Eireag (Beauty), or Aighneann (Lover), or Gort (Sourness); he has nigh as many names as he has faces. What will you call him, Brigit of the Judgments?"

Brigit of the Judgments turned a hungry face to meet her guest's clear eyes.

"He is the child I lost long ago," she muttered, "he is my little Culainn, and he has his father's eyes—there never was a comelier lad than my Eoghan: and because his dead beauty kept the door of my heart I never kissed the lips of thy father, Brigit, good mate though he made me. Let me have the child, daughter of the stranger: he is mine." Kathaleen Ny-Houlahan smiled. "Told I not that he was Moran of the many names? Now," turning to the youngest Brigit, "tell me what he seemeth to thee, O little maiden of the yellow cool?" And the third Brigit drew back with a face that blossomed red as the leaves at a rose's heart.

"I see—" she said, and put back the yellow hair that the wind blew in her face, "I see— Oh mother I see what you saw in Eoghan's face—and now shall I say all that I see? I see short joy and long sorrow, shame and severance and suffering, patience and pride—and do I not also see that I would thole the sorrow for the sake of the short joy? Oh mother, hold me fast lest I gather the shame, too."

"I said," quoth Kathaleen Ny-Houlahan, "that he was Moran of the many names. Aongus or Aighneann wouldst thou call him, O little one? and to thy mother is he her lost child and her lost husband: and what to me? Ah, when last I looked him in the face, I called him Conasg (War): for I saw a light in his eyes that was like the light of swords. And now, O old mother, rise up and say what thou seest in his face."

"I am blind, Lady," muttered Brigit the Farmer. "I am blind and I cannot see."

"Rise up," said Kathaleen Ny-Houlahan, as if she had not heard, "and look on him, and say what thou seest in his face."

So the old woman rose and came to her side, without help of either staff or guiding hand, and she fixed her blind eyes on the face asleep on the breast of Kathaleen Ny-Houlahan. Then to the watching mother and daughter it seemed that the blind eyes gathered colour and depth as they gazed: and last, the light that had left them. And then with a cry the grandmother fell back into Brigit of the Judgments' arms, and women came from the house and bore her in, and laid her softly on her bed, seeing that she was stricken with death. And Brigit of the Judgments wept over the happy face of her gray mother, and never heeded that she hindered her soul from passing: and, outside in the winter sunshine, Kathaleen Ny-Houlahan waited with her back against the holy whitethorn. And beside her the youngest Brigit stood, dreaming, looking past bawn and barn away to the silvery ribbon of the Boyne running swiftly away to wooded Brugh where Aongus Oge was still thought to have his golden house. And Kathaleen Ny-Houlahan turned her eyes on the girl's face, and, holding them there, again she turned back the mantle from the face of him she bore on her bosom. And softly she said, "Look!" and Brigit obeyed her. And as she looked, there came a smile over the sleeping face, and the smile smote to the girl's heart with sorrow as sharp as a spear: but Kathaleen's look kept back the tears from her eyes and the cry from her lips: and for a little while the twain kept silence. And then Kathaleen covered the sleeping face, and with that Brigit's tongue was loosed, and she cried out, sobbing, "Oh! fair he is and dear he is, Dark Woman, and a while since would I have died to walk the world with him: and now it seems to be better to live and die without him—and that your frowns were dearer than his praising, Beauty of the World!"

"I am not she!" said Kathaleen Ny-Houlahan. "She passes away, and I can never die—for even when my own children stone me, I must rise again, and go on my road. And—oh! Flesh of my flesh, but you have stoned me often!" she cried. "And oh! but how good it were to feel the shamrocks growing over me!"

"But then the world would end, Pulse of our hearts," said Brigit. "And must you go on your way again, you and Moran of the many names? Will you not stay a little—and we would serve you well?"

"It is for me to serve my people," said Kathaleen. "But I must not stay: for I was born when the wandering wind met the wandering fire, and the twain are in my blood."

"Then take me with you," Brigit cried, "for I shall never be wife or mother, and what use is there for me in my mother's house? Take me with you, Heart of hearts, and let me wander, too, till I die."

"Brigit the Farmer served me well in her eighty years, and never she served me better than when she milked her kine in the byres of Conor the King. And well has Brigit your mother served me, and all the better for the loss of her fair Eoghan: and when your father Senchan sang before Conor MacNessa, he was serving me, though he knew it not. And now," said Kathaleen Ny-Houlahan, "do you also serve me, Brigit. My daughters dwell in their father's houses, and see the green lands pass to the thriftless man and the hard man: and are they better than hostages even in their husbands' houses? Go out and cry shame till this thing cease, my Brigit: till the women that have no brothers take the wasted lands and deal gently by them. Cry out—and cry loudly, though every Brehon in the land say you nay: Conor MacNessa has ears to hear."

Then she turned and went, and young Brigit stood alone under the thorn-tree, making ready for the task laid upon her: and from the house came the voice of women keening for the dead, but very softly, lest they should wake the dreadful hounds that lie in wait to catch the naked soul. But they might have shrieked their shrillest, for the soul of Brigit the Farmer walked safely in the shadow of Kathaleen Ny-Houlahan.

Silk of the Kine.

Silk of the Kine.

Silk of the kine, do not those great waves grow
Weary of lashing granite shores of thine,
Shores that decay and death will never know,
    Silk of the kine?

Are not thy soft eyes tired of shade and shine,
And thy kind lips a-weary, drinking so,
For many years a black and bitter wine?
Take comfort, Gra Machree: the years are slow,
Yet bring the day (tho' not for eyes of mine)
When thou shalt rise up crowned above thy foe,
    Silk of the kine!

Cuchullin's Belt.

CUCHULLIN'S BELT.

Now Cuchullin—the Hound of Murthemney—the beloved of the Dé Danann gods—had a fair wife and a noble, named Eimer, and he loved her well: and a fairy mistress he had also, and when his dreams took him he loved the Shee lady, Fand, more heartily than, waking, he had ever loved Eimer, his wife. But waking or dreaming, he was the goodliest man that ever lived, and the fairest to see: and so thought many another besides Eimer. Now this Eimer was a great lady and a noted housewife, and she kept her maidens busy all day, spinning and weaving and combing, so that there was little rest in her greenan, from the women working at the top wool and the noil or short wool, to Eimer herself gathering up the skeins of finished yarn, and the skeins of fine yellow silk.

"Ye must work more steadily, my women," said Eimer, weighing first the silk in her hands, and then the yarn, "for here is less weight than yesterday. Ineen of Orgiall, look how thy web is spoiled."

"Ineen is weaving the web of her own life," laughed the other women: but Eimer frowned as she watched the Golden Hostage send her shuttle through the crooked weft. Now the Golden Hostage was a tall maiden, and deep-bosomed, and the naked arms and throat clasped with the gold chains of Orgiall hostages, were shapely, although the sun had changed their white to brown: and the hair of her hung down to her knee like a black cloud, and the lips of her were as red as quickenberries, and the eyes of her were gray, like the sea. And, seeing that she was young and comely to see, the lady Eimer frowned and darkened, for her heart was as full of jealousy as ever the heart of Oisin was full of song: yet she herself was a fair woman and a stately, and not one among her women could match her feet in the dance or her fingers on the tympan.

"Be diligent," she said, frowning, "there is yet an hour of light, and then may ye sit idle in the greenan."

"She goeth to meet her husband," whispered the women, as she crossed the threshold, "and he is new from dreams of Tir na n'Og and of the Woman of the Shee, belike. Ho! brown girl, how speeds thy weaving now?"

"I pray you let me be:" said the Orgiallan, weaving away, "since half my work is to do."

But the women would not be still: and their chatter broke out again, like the sound of a little running stream.

"Ho! brown girl, dost think thou weavest Eimer's shroud, that thou weavest so faithfully?"

"Or Cuchullin's bridal shirt?" laughed another. "There goes her shuttle all at random."

"We heard that thou hadst a lover in Orgiall, brown girl: and that he was wise in Druid arts. How came it that he let thee go to Eimer's house to walk thy feet lame on alien roads, and to have thy wrists weighed down with golden fetters? How came it so?

"Weave thy best, and our lady will give thee in marriage to Conall the bard: his second wife is dead: and he likes well to wed among the women of Eimer's household."

So they mocked her: Una, Gormshuil, Orfla, Niam, and Onoir: and they laughed and chanted mocking rhymes around her, and still the Orgiallan wove on, and made as if she heard them not. But presently she left her web, and went across the greenan to cool her hot hands with fresh water, and her comrades gathered round her work, silent at first. For in the purple web she had woven figures of men and women and dogs: and at first the meaning of the figures took them not, and when it reached beyond their eyes their knowledge kept them silent. For on the web the Orgiallan had worked a wolf-hound sleeping in the arms of a woman whose robe was of the elfin green, and behind the twain there rose a wild figure that was like the lady Eimer's when anger shook her beauty from her.

Then said Onoir, "Thou hast courage, Orgiallan, and if she kills thee for this, I will lay gesa on my brother to revenge thee."

And Una, "Take up that courage in thine hands, Hostage, and win out from this house: for if thou abidest Eimer's coming, surely thy next need will be for the baked clay urn and the stone kistvaen."

And "Go!" said all the rest, with one voice. "Cover thy saffron gown with yonder cloak, and thine head with a kerchief, and thou mayest pass without any knowing that thou art not Caitlin the herd-woman or More the hen-wife, for both be of thy height."

"I go not," said the Orgiallan, quietly. "Fall back, companions, and let our mistress pass." And she sat down again to her web, and waited while the women scattered right and left before Eimer, as she crossed the greenan, stately in her garments of blue and saffron, and looked on the woven picture of her husband's beguiling. "Thou hast a pretty wit, O golden maid," she said, when she had looked her fill, "and a pretty skill with the shuttle when thou pleasest. And so thou wert once plighted to a warlock—ay? of our own island?"

"Of Dane-land," Ineen the Hostage answered, gravely.

"It is well," Eimer said, slowly and softly. "Didst thou love him, brown girl? as well as I love Cuchullin?"

"As well."

"Weave me a magic belt, then: and weave it cunningly and well, thou Golden Hostage, and it may be I shall send thee home to thy lover. Or it may be I shall give thee to the stones in Carrownamaddoo, the quarter of the dogs."

"How shall I weave the belt?"

"Thou knowest, Beauty of the World," Eimer said, bitterly. "'Tis a small thing to ask of a warlock's mistress." Ineen smiled, as she drew out a knife from her girdle and cut off a great lock of her heavy hair.

"I must have gold hair, too," she said. "Mistress, wilt thou bid Onoir or Orfla give me of their locks? Nay, but Onoir is too dark. Orfla's is of the true honey-colour." And then she went to the weaving again, and it was midnight before she laid her shuttle down, and flung over Eimer's arm the finished work of woven hair, soft and fine and wonderful to look upon.

"Thy will is done, my mistress," she said, "and henceforward the magic girdle will keep far from Cuchullin the dreams that Fand sends." The knife lay at her feet now, and Eimer snatched it and struck for the girl's heart: but her aim was ill, and yet Ineen had stood still to take the blow. "Thy lover's Dhouls have saved thee for to-night," Eimer said, furiously, "but to-morrow is mine. Go thou and sleep and gather thy force up for to-morrow: and hope not to escape, daughter of a witch, for bower and bawn are guarded by my husband's men."

And Ineen laughed as she went to her sleeping-place: but Eimer's eyes were dark with fear as she held the knife to the torch-light, for the stain upon it was the stain, not of blood, but of sea-water. And the next day, folk sought high and low for Ineen, but found her not: and they whispered among themselves that she came and went as she would by means of black magic, and that belike the tale was true which told that her father Malachi of the Clan Colla had taken a sea-woman to wife.

But, nevertheless, the next day Cuchullin wore the magic girdle: and Fand visited him in his dreams no more. And when seven days had gone by, Eimer heard him moan beside her in the night, and when she asked what ailed him, he said, heavily, "I am dream-stolen, and now my sleep is gone from me, my wife, and I shall go mad and die. This thing has been done me by an enemy. Wife, knowest thou any herb to give me ease?"

"To-morrow I will go out into the fields," she said, "and we will snare a nightingale and lay its heart under thy head as thou liest, and thus will sleep surely come to thee, if the kind gods grant that no wind blows."

But the root of Cuchullin's ill lay deeper yet, and for two more nights he lay and wrestled hard to hold sleep with him, but with no success: and on the third morning he rose up, with a darkness in his eyes and a noise in his ears that held him from knowing Eimer when she clung to him and strove to hold him back. But she did not loose the girdle, for her fear lest he should dream of Fand was greater than her fear for Cuchullin. And for a day and a night Cuchullin went seawards, smiting boughs and tree-stems as he went, in his madness, and presently he stood upon the sands and fought with the sea, striking the subsiding waters now with his sword, and now with his bare hands. And as the tide turned, there leapt to his side a woman with black hair lifting in the wind, and strand by strand she tore from him the girdle of woman's hair, and as the last lock tore apart, the madness departed from Cuchullin and he slept. And Ineen sat beside him on the sand, holding his head on her knees: and presently he awoke in midmost of a dream of the Fairy woman, hearing a voice sobbing in his ears.

"I wove the belt to thine undoing, and I broke the belt to thine undoing. And mine own people come against thee for the blows thy madness struck. Rise, lord, and fight for thy life, and let thy dreams be. Bite, Hound: for thy chain is snapped." And Cuchullin started up, and saw wave after wave coming a-land, full of threatening faces and shaken spears, and he took his sword from Ineen's hands, and made ready to fight the sea. And, fighting blindly with the sea-folk, he felt presently the grip of many hands upon him, and he was dragged to his knees, and he heard voices mocking him. "Where is thy strength, O great champion? Gone with the belt that kept thy dreams aloof? Yield thee, then, Cu———, and let the Hound be taken in leash to his kennel. Thanks, Ineen Dhu, for the broken girdle."

"But the girdle is here," Ineen cried : and Cuchullin felt her arms clasped about his body. "Give back, O sea-people: what girdle is so strong as a girdle of flesh and blood?"

"The other girdle," shrilled the sea-people back. "The girdle of dead hands, O Ineen : and that he cannot win. Give back and let us drown him."

Cuchullin's dreams swept round him now : but in spite of them he knew that the waves were breaking against his breast, and that Ineen's arms were tightening about him : and twixt sleep and waking he looked down at her as she clung to him, and listened, wondering, to the stream of song that poured from her open lips. And with the last word of her song there rose a long shriek of sorrow from the sea-people, and a wave lifted Cuchullin and Ineen, and brought them gently to shore. And when next Cuchullin woke from his dreams he found that Ineen still held him fast, though she was dead and cold : and with some difficulty he loosed her hands from him, and dug with his sword a grave for her in the sand, and there he laid her sorrowfully, praying Angus, the Master of Love, to keep her soul in his Golden House, and Manannan Mac Lir to hold his waves aloof from her sleeping-place. And when he visited the place with Eimer after a year and a day, they found that the sea had fallen back for half a league, and that the place where the sea-girl slept was a broad space of grass, and in the midst of the grass rose white spikes of meadowsweet, the flower which for the sake of a forgotten love and a forgotten sacrifice is called of us to-day Crios Chu-chulainn (Cuchullin's Belt).

A Connaught Lament.

A Connaught Lament.

I will arise and go hence to the west,
And dig me a grave where the hill-winds call;
But O were I dead, were I dust, the fall
Of my own love's footstep would break my rest!

My heart in my bosom is black as a sloe!
I heed not cuckoo, nor wren, nor swallow:
Like a flying leaf in the sky's blue hollow
The heart in my breast is, that beats so low.

Because of the words your lips have spoken,
(O dear black head that I must not follow)
My heart is a grave that is stripped and hollow,
As ice on the water my heart is broken.

O lips forgetful and kindness fickle,
The swallow goes south with you: I go west
Where fields are empty and scythes at rest.
I am the poppy and you the sickle;
My heart is broken within my breast.

The Lamp of Brighid.

THE LAMP OF BRIGHID.

FEVER and famine were in the country of Tirconnell, and betwixt these two fires the people forgot the gods: women turning their faces to the wall, and dying with never a prayer, while men held up accusing hands to the blank blue skies, and cursed Kasar among the gods of the Fomoroh, and Lug and Dagdé of the Dé Dananns. Even the Shee were neglected, and everywhere the Vanitha (mistress of the house) forgot to scatter crumbs and spill drops of milk upon her threshold for Dark Joan and Oonah and Cleena and Donn of the Sandhills: and the little People went hungry past the closed doors at twilight, while within the famished human things made short work of the thin milk and the poor bread. At last even the lights in the great House of Brighid went out one by one as, one by one, the holy women died of hunger or plague, till at last there was left alight only one of all the gold and silver lamps, and just as this one lamp had been refilled and lighted before the great carved image of Brighid, sitting with a huge golden book open on her knees—just as the scented oil gave out its odour of pine—the last recluse dropped her oil-cruse and fell dead at the feet of the holy statue. Some good women, coming to do hopeless worship to holy Brighid, found her lying there, and having done the last kind offices for her, and laid her with hurried prayers in the common grave of her sisters, went back to their hungry homes, leaving the door of the shrine wide open. Presently there came two small figures timidly across the threshold, and so into the deserted holy place—a boy and girl dressed in mere rags for all the cold March wind that whistled outside, twin children whose dead mother had mocked at holy Brighid a-dying, and whose living father would have torn down her very shrine if his hands had been as strong as his hatred.

"Breed," said the boy, lifting his gentle blind eyes from the ground, "where's the wind that I feel blowing?"

"It comes from the open door," Breed answered hurriedly, "and never a stir will it stir for all my pushing—bad cess to it for a stubborn door! And the blessed lamp will be blown out altogether, Maurice, unless we can do something to save it."

"There's the lamp at home," Maurice said slowly, "and it's full of oil, Breed. You might run and fetch it here, machree, and light it from the blessed lamp yonder. I'll wait till you come."

"Will you? It's lonely here," little Breed said, warningly. "'Tis a mile home and a mile back, and the hunger makes me run slower than I used."

"Set me close to the holy lady Brighid," Maurice McCaura said, smiling, "where I can touch her with my hands: and then ye can go, Breed; I'll be safe enough in Brighid's own house." Breed led him forward a step or two, and guided his hands till they touched the feet of Brighid's image; then she turned and her bare feet pattered softly down the dusty aisle, across the threshold and out into the sparse pale sunshine outside. Her blind brother stood still where she had placed him, clinging to Brighid's golden feet: and presently, when they began to quiver and move under his clinging fingers, he stood, if possible, even stiller than before.

"Who holds my feet?" said a deep sweet voice. "Who, of all my children?"

"It's Maurice McCaura," the boy said,

faintly. "Lady Brighid, will you give us bread? Breed and Michael and my father are hungry, and baby Caitlin's dead: and there's the black Death in nearly every home in Munster."

"And yourself, child?"

"I'm not so hungry now," the boy whispered. "It's Breed—and—and little Michael —and there's no bread in the house, and no potatoes in the kish—"

"How many mouths to feed?" said the deep voice.

"Three, Lady Brighid. Will you feed them?" pleaded the blind lad.

"And yours is the fourth. Hark.—Now would you like to give bread to the children's hungry mouths, and to your father's? Will you give yourself to me to be my servant, child?"

"Yes," said Maurice quietly. Two strong gentle arms closed round his slight body now and lifted him from the ground—lifted and held him breast-high, till he felt the goddess's breath warm upon his blind eyes.

"Breed and Michael and your father shall have food this very day—and Breed shall not grieve long for you: I promise that," Brighid said gently. "Now, child, let me seal you to my service." She held him to her bosom and kissed his blind eyes with soft cold kisses, until the dull hunger pain and the fluttering heart stopped together; and Breed, come back and lighting her lamp from the sacred light, found only a dead boy awaiting her, at the feet of holy Brighid. There was but little moan made over Maurice McCaura; even Breed, who loved him better than herself, watched him buried in his mother's grave with very few tears, and those not tears of bitterness. Smiles and tears were not plentiful with Breed henceforward: the moonlight quiet of her small white face was not disturbed for her drunken father, or Michael, rosy and romping when the fever and famine ceased as suddenly as they had come; her whole care was for the lamp she had lighted from the one which had long ago burned out in Brighid's temple, and whose flame she nursed and tended, as other girls and women tended the fire of another Brighid, in a house under mighty oak-trees at Cill-dara. Days and weeks went by, and months merged into years: and old Michael McCaura dug a grave for young Michael in another year of famine: and Breed came to her seventeenth year.

And it fell to her lot to find a shadow at her side wherever she went, and to have a voice in her ears, that whispered of love and gladness: and Breed learned to blush and tremble like other girls, but still she was faithful to her chosen work of tending the holy fire of goddess Brighid. There came a day, however, when the lover turned from Breed's moonlight to the lilies and roses of a better-dowered maiden : and another day yet there came, when a fall of earth from the mountain-side buried bride and groom and half a score of wedding guests in one common grave, to which came Breed with her lamp at dead of night, toiling with bleeding and bruised hands till she had cleared the earth from the two faces in the world that she most loved and most hated. Other hands drew them out and gave them holy burial, not Breed's; she and her lamp vanished from the eyes of men when she had looked upon those two dead faces: and only now and then a dreamy colleen sees a slender figure gliding among the trees on a misty night with a lighted lamp of quaint shape held high in her hand. And the girl who sees this figure of Breed, however glad her love may be, and however true her lover, will never be wife or mother, but like Breed's her life will be broken and sorrowful here, though it may be made beautiful and complete in Tir na n'Og, in the service of Brighids three, whose names are **Law** and **Wisdom** and **Love**.

Ros Geal Dhu.

Ros Geal Dhu.

A greeting, Dark Rose, where thou sittest a-spinning,
A thread without ending, and without beginning:
A thread of all colours, gold, purple, and blue:
Dark Rose,'neath thy thorn-tree, how wears the day through?

" My day it wears onward 'twixt spinning and weaving,
The noise of men's laughter, the cry of their grieving
Drifts slow by my thorn-tree like drifting of snow,
And on the old branches the new blossoms blow.

" I heed not the sorrow, nor mock at the laughter,
I weave the white sark and the yellow veil after:
I have trodden the grapes, I have pressed out the wine,
And all men shall drink of this vintage of mine.

" One snatches the laurel I twined for his brother,
One kisses my feet: I heed one nor another:
Am I Death, O my children, or Life! Can ye tell — ?
Or the ghost of maid Truth that was drowned in her well?"

Crióch Agus Amen.

CRÍOCH AGUS AMEN.

THE END: and Amen.

Someone has carved these words on a weather-beaten wooden cross in Sid Cruachan: and when I was last in Connaught I learned the story to which they form the tag. Here it is: told as it was told to me by an old, old man who might perhaps have been Ocaill, once a king of the gentle folk in Connaught.

Once upon a time the Hungry Death lay heavy upon Connaught, and everywhere in the glens and hollows there grew up the Fairgurtha: the Hungry Grass which marks where graceless men have eaten and drank their fill, and never thought of scattering drop or crumb for the "gentle" folk: and the Hungry Death lay long heavily upon Connaught, so that corn and kine and people died, and men and kine lay in one deep ditch for all grave. That is to say, the poor folk: but the rich had full barns and brimming coffers, and the Hungry Death held off from them so long that they thought

He dared not touch them. But one of their number thought differently: and he went down among the dying and dead with food and comfort and prayers: and when milk and meat were of no use, he brought holy water and blessed candles, and the last offices of prayer and spade he did them, and then turned sadly homewards. Priest, soldier, and student were his three brothers, and there was no help in any of them at this time, for Donat was busy courting a lady of the Pale, and Anthony was buried in his rare missals, and Gildea was away in Rome in the train of my lord Cardinal d'Este. His father had no will to help him, and his mother, who would have sold her last jewel for charity's sake, had long been a saint in heaven: therefore it fell to Gilchrist to labour alone, and the long days dragged on to autumn: and each took a thread of hope with them. One day Anthony the student came down from among his books and sought out Gilchrist, with a new look of purpose in his grave face.

"I have read the stars for seven nights now, brother," he said, "and seven times I have looked in my crystal ball at daybreak, and crystal and stars say the same thing, Gilchrist; the Devil is in the mask of the Hungry Death. Go down and bid them set the chapel-bells a-ringing."

"What use?" Gilchrist said. "Does your crystal show you how one might meet the Hungry Death face to face, Anthony?"

"Yes," Anthony said, slowly. "It is a meeting I have long desired, Gilchrist: and I have tried many spells to bring the Dark Man to me. What charms did the people use, think you, that the Hungry Death has come to *them*, and taken no heed of me?"

"What will you ask of him, Anthony, when you see him face to face?"

"Ask—what I have desired all the thirty years of my life, Gilchrist: the philosopher's stone."

"No other richer gift?" Gilchrist asked, laughing into Anthony's eager face. "Not all the kingdoms of the world, my brother? Not the ghost of Helen that Dr. Faustus desired? Not the ring of Gyges?"

"No," Anthony said, "Helen could not give me the philosopher's stone: and what is one man's soul weighed with that?"

"Is the stone so heavy, then?" Gilchrist asked, with eyes that sparkled suddenly. "Anthony, if your mind is set on seeing the Prince o' the Air, let me bide with you."

"I am not afraid," Anthony said coldly. "But you can stand by, Gilchrist, an you choose. He will be like any Court gentleman belike, with a dainty ruff and a rose in his ear, and a good Toledo blade."

And so it fell out. The charms were spoken, and a pinch of shining powder scattered into the brazier, and, with no scent of sulphur or burst of blue flame, the door of Anthony's chamber swung open, and a dapper gentleman in a velvet cloak entered and saluted the brothers with all the grace of France.

"Are you the Hungry Death" Gilchrist asked, since Anthony did not speak, but sat huddled up in his chair shivering as if he were cold. The visitor bowed. "My eke-name for the present, Messer," he said. "May I confer one on you since your given name offends me? A thousand thanks. Then, Dov, what would you have of me? and you, Dav?" looking at Anthony with smiling eyes.

"Let the learned man speak while the ox listens," Gilchrist said, keeping his grave eyes on those that smiled. "Anthony—" but Anthony did not speak.

"He is taking counsel of fear," said the visitor gaily. "Well, Dov, do thou take counsel also. "I have done so," Gilchrist said. "I desire to know when the Hungry Death goes back to his own place." The visitor's smiling face sharpened and grew fierce. "When I have souls enough," he snarled. "There are more stones than souls in Connaught, and, Dov you hinder me from taking my own. Take heed lest I find a goad for you, good ox."

"I will hinder you more before that goad is pointed," Gilchrist said. "When will your shadow lift from us, Dark Man? What will you take to go?"

"The souls of old Anthony Sheehy, and his sons Anthony and Donat and Gil the priest." Then the guest threw back his head and laughed shrilly. "And where shall I find them, Dov? Old Anthony's heart is a wine-cup, and Gil the priest's is a warren of feeble coney-sins, and young Anthony's is a book with painted edges, and nothing writ on the pages—and Donat's heart is a ruby trinket for mistress Adeliza's breast. Whither shall I go look for the souls they used to have? Even my wisdom fails to see them in any place within my ken."

"Does it so?" Gilchrist said. "Can perhaps my folly help out your worship's wisdom, at a pinch?"

"Sell me your soul, and we will see."

"And what then?"

"Why then— Come, I will deal generously with you, merchant though I be—and I am tired of hunting weasel-souls over Connaught. Give me your soul, and they shall not see the Hungry Death again, they, nor their children's children. My word is my bond, outcast though you call me: the Hungry Death shall go, when your soul is mine."

"What will you do with it?" Gilchrist asked. The other laughed a thin laugh.

"Cut souls out of it for your father and your brothers—and one, mayhap, for the lady Adeliza. Then—when they die, I shall have all the kin: all."

"Except my mother," Gilchrist said quietly. "Take my soul then, and do with it as you will." The visitor held out his hand, and clasped Gilchrist's for a long minute: then their hands fell apart, and Gilchrist heard Anthony's voice speak sharply in his ears.

"Was it a dream or no? Gilchrist, tell me!"

"It was a dream," Gilchrist said, gently. "It is not well to sleep by the open window at twilight, Anthony, for the air from the marshes is heavy with mist."

"I dreamed that I was dead," Anthony said, shivering. "I think the Hungry Death must ha' touched me, passing by."

"Perhaps," Gilchrist said. "I think he will not pass by again. Shall we go down, Anthony? I hear Donat calling us."

So they went down to a changed life for both. For the Hungry Death had killed its last victim, and henceforward the people found that old Anthony Sheehy's coffers were readier to open than of old, and that young Anthony would read the fortunes of their absent dear ones in his crystal ball, or fill a vial with some unknown liquid that cured cramps more swiftly than the expressed juice of mullein and marjoram: and so they grew used to turning in their lesser troubles to others than the man who only had helped them in their bitterest need. And Gilchrist was well pleased to know that his sacrifice had quickened the charity of his kindred : and the memory of the sacrifice itself was not able to alter his life materially outwardly or inwardly. Only as years went on he grew a little graver and less quick to smile, but always his hands were ready to salve and serve though now he was slower to pray beside the sick-beds, not altogether because of the pain that pierced him at each holy word he uttered. But when the need was sorest he was ready with the help or the prayer: though for himself he never prayed. And when Donat's eldest son was ten years old, and student Anthony was seated in soldier Anthony's place, and Gildea had put off his black cassock for a scarlet gown, then Gilchrist fell sick of some nameless disease, and lay for months with all his body dead save the kindly heart and the busy brain: having lain long thus it fell to him to see Donat gathered to his fathers of a sudden fever, and Donat's eldest son brought in dead and drowned from a rowing-match with other lads of his degree.

So it came to pass that Donat's second son, young Gilchrist, became heir to the Tir-na-Sheoghaidh (the Sheehys' country) : and on the day that Cathal was buried Gilchrist sent for Gildea to come to his chamber when he had made an end of striving to comfort Cathal's mother for her newest loss. So Gildea came, and listened to Gilchrist's confession, and when it was at an end he sat for a long time with his face hidden in his hands. And presently lifting up his head he spoke as the Cardinal :

"I cannot shrive you, Gilchrist Sheehy, and I dare not bless you, who have sold your soul. But you sold it for God's love, Gilchrist, and one of the kindred whose souls are yours loves you the better for it. Our souls are yours —and since you sold it for a selfless cause, Gilchrist, it seems to me the pact is null and void : that the Dark Man therefore has power upon none of us."

"Upon none of *you*," Gilchrist said quietly. "If I have given my soul among my kindred I have none to save or lose, Gildea : and so what end is there to this journey that I go upon ?"

"I do not know," Gildea said. "What comfort can I give you?"

"I can go comfortless," Gilchrist said smiling. "I have looked this end in the face a many years, Gildea. So when they bury me write nothing of my kindred nor even my name, but put upon the stone the words scribes write at the end of their tales and verses."

That night he died: and that the Cardinal obeyed his last wish the cross shows. But I cannot help believing that the priest's logic and Gilchrist's belief were alike wrong: and that nothingness is *not* the end of that bargain made in the Joyces' country some three hundred and odd years ago. Even if it were, such an end might possibly be worth more than the immortality of Claudio.

The Wind Among the Reeds.

The Wind Among the Reeds.

Mavrone, Mavrone! the wind among the reeds.
It calls and cries, and will not let me be;
And all its cry is of forgotten deeds
When men were loved of all the Daoine-sidhe.

O Shee that have forgotten how to love,
And Shee that have forgotten how to hate,
Asleep 'neath quicken boughs that no winds move,
Come back to us ere yet it be too late.

Pipe to us once again, lest we forget
What piping means, till all the Silver Spears
Be wild with gusty music, such as met
Carolan once, amid the dusty years.

Dance in your rings again: the yellow weeds
You used to ride so far, mount as of old—
Play hide and seek with winds among the reeds,
And pay your scores again with fairy gold.

Boholaun and I.

BOHOLAUN AND I.

BOHOLAUN stands up stiff and uncomely now in the pitiless morning sunshine—a mere stalk of ragweed, and nothing more—but let twilight once come up from the land of the Shee, and work her wild will with these familiar fields of Lismahoga, and Boholaun will alter beyond recognition, putting off rough leaf and ragged flower for a shining silken coat of elfin grey, and a flowing mane and tail of hair fine as woven glass, and moonshine coloured. Then unseen hands will lead him softly out from the fairy-ring where he stands all day, and unseen feet will press his silken sides till his stride outpaces the wind itself, and his silver hoofs leave shining tracks west on the cliffs of Galway, and east in the Wexford sands. Is it Boholaun that has changed, or only I, or have I unwittingly crossed the fairy-ring? Still he stands up erect and unbeautiful, but deep down under the earth I hear the ringing of elfin bridles, and the stamping of fairy hoofs: and now the green-coated figures are swarming about me, and the air is drowsy with the whirr of their wings—or is it a fairy song? It is strange and sleepy and sweet, and now that it has fallen silent I am hungering to hear it again, and yet ——

Oh! I am awake now, and lonely for lack of the flittering figures, and the elfin song, and the gallant steed that stood up in Boholaun's place, scraping the ground with an impatient hoof. I am awake, but I remember that wild ride with Boholaun, and I hasten to set it down on paper ere the memory of it leaves me quite.

If I mounted him voluntarily, or if unseen hands helped me to the saddle, I do not know: but that I was on his back is as true as that I now stand dismounted.

Lough and valley flashed by us, a medley of green and grey, and next, sharp spears of mountains glorious with sunset: after that a blinding mist, and then a flash of pearl and rose that may have been a gate, and then—Ah! *then!* Asleep or awake, I slid from the saddle, and sank at the feet of a great and gracious figure, robed with mist. And as I lay at her feet, other figures came and closed about me, grave and splendid and stately, looking at me with eyes that probed my soul; till I felt naked and ashamed as Adam did in Eden. I put my hands before my face to shield it, but their looks went deeper down than my eyes, and my soul I could not shield as I could my face. And in the scathing white light of their looks, sins great and small, sins remembered and sins forgotten, sins repented and sins cherished, raised their ugly heads, and made me shrink and quiver and recoil from their foulness, while a light kiss slid from a dusky corner of my heart, and showed itself a full-grown snake, and an idle lie collapsed to a thing lamentable in its vanity and hideousness. And still they looked at me with eyes terrible in their mute reproach, and no word came from their folded lips, till once more the misty woman's figure bent over me, and scalding tears fell from her eyes on my upturned face. And after that a voice broke the dreadful tension of the silence. "Diarmuid!" It let in a light upon my soul more scathing than that in which I had lain before: and I leapt to my feet, stung with intolerable pain, and answered to the name which had been mine and now was not. And the voice called again in a broken and tearful fashion, "Diarmuid! Diarmuid!" And I flung out my hands in an anguish of appeal, and other hands caught them, and drew me softly into a long embrace. I could not see the eyes that wept over me, or the lips whose breath stirred my hair, but seeing is not knowledge: and I had never quite forgotten Grainne, though ages had been blown down the wind since our arms held each other last. Yet I was not glad to know her arms about me again. I cried out, and struggled to escape from them, because I was burning with intolerable shame.

"No, no, no!" I cried, not knowing what I denied. And the arms held me fast: and the soft voice crooned "Diarmuid!" and at last I gathered strength to know what I sought to deny, and in set words I said: "It was not I who loved you, Grainne, in days when you were Fionn's wife and Diarmuid's betrothed. Some other man: not I."

And those that stood round laughed, all save the woman who had greeted me first, Kásar the Fomorian Queen; and she sobbed. Then from denial I passed to questioning.

"Was it you for whom I have hungered all my life—you, Grainne, and no other?"

"I, Grainne: and no other."

"But look at me," I cried, "a man grown, and yet as weak as a child, Grainne, and marred after a fashion that makes children point after me in the streets. Take your eyes away, and let me die here!"

"Look!" she said, and I looked where her finger pointed, and saw a man standing before me, dressed in some barbaric, antique fashion, with gold on the shield he held, and a glimmer of gold in his dusky hair. And I was ashamed before my old self, and my eyes smarted with tears I could not shed. But Grainne's voice was sweet in my ears again as she said—" I hold you in my arms, one and the same with him you look upon—not two as you fancy now : but the body of Maurice Cahill holds the soul of Diarmuid, and Grainne is weary till the twain come to her."

Then there were no more faces before my eyes, but only flashing water, and sweeps of turf, and crags where the eagles nest, and know naught of the Shee and their "old ever-busy moneyed land," as Boholaun swept me back to my old life and my old burden, and the old cold, clear daylight of this world where the Shee are not seen of us awake. I think I do my worldly part no worse for my one glimpse of Tir na n' Og, and the hope that keeps my heart warm night and day—the hope that some day I may fling off this body whereof I am so weary, and re-assume my old shape and my old name. And if this come to pass, I do not doubt—for all he stands a mere dry weed again in the midst of the fairy-ring—I do not doubt that Boholaun, rather than any other guide, will come to carry me back to the Land of Youth—to my old self—and to *Grainne*.

The Fairy Fiddler.

The Fairy Fiddler.

'Tis I go fiddling, fiddling,
   By weedy ways forlorn :
I make the blackbird's music
   Ere in his breast 'tis born :
The sleeping larks I waken
   Twixt the midnight and the morn.

No man alive has seen me,
   But women hear me play
Sometimes at door or window,
   Fiddling the souls away,—
The child's soul and the colleen's
   Out of the covering clay.

None of my fairy kinsmen
   Make music with me now :
Alone the raths I wander
   Or ride the whitethorn bough
But the wild swans they know me,
   And the horse that draws the plough.

Daluan.

DALUAN.

IT was in Galway that I met him first: a slim lad in a rough frieze suit, crossing the quaking bog-edge with perfect serenity and carelessness, and never once looking to see where he set his bare brown feet.

"Save you kindly," he called back in answer to my "God save you," leapt nimbly to the solid ground where I stood, and fell to arranging a bit of bog-cotton in the curious scarlet cap he wore. I had no intention of glancing inquisitively at his bare feet, but I suppose I must have done so, for, without looking up, he said in a perfectly level voice, "Oh, I have odds and ends of civilisation about me after all, see." He produced from the satchel on his shoulders a neat pair of brogues, composedly sitting down on a tuft of grass to put them on, and, rising, looked at me for the first time with a pair of roguish eyes, so darkly blue that they looked black.

"Shall we join company? You are going to Galway." I answered it as a question, though it was more an assertion.

"Yes: I am going there."

"Right: so am I. Do you speak Irish?"

"No, worse luck! though I am Irish-born."

"You are a Browne of Carlow, I think," said my companion, stepping out with a light swinging step. "Well," scarcely listening to my surprised assent, "I can speak Saxon to you. Have the bees of Carlow their stings still? I suppose not."

"You are proverb-wise, I see," I said, somewhat piqued. "Since you know my name I might as well know yours—I'm afraid I cannot guess it." He faced round on me, guessing perhaps that I was annoyed, and held out a hand delicate and slender as a lady's. "I am too light for you to quarrel with," he answered. "Nobody runs amuck at the thistledown even when it flies into folks' faces. Well. . . . I am lighter than the thistledown, and idler: and my name's Daluan. "I took the proffered hand and found it icy cold to my touch, though as soft as the thistledown he had likened himself to. Then he drew it away from me with a laugh, and we proceeded on our way to Galway town, I not a little speculative as to the character of my odd companion, and he, quite cool and composed, singing a wild Irish song as he went.

"All away to Tir na n'Og are many roads that run,
But the darkest road is trodden of the King of Ireland's son."

"Do you see that?" he said presently, pointing to a cairn on the roadside. "There lies one of those that liked well to see the green above the red: a good Irishman, and a kind soul, for all his empty pockets and waste lands. And one day men that he had fed and sheltered came and shot him on his own doorstep, and left him to the tender mercies of the kites."

"Who buried him here, then?" I enquired sharply. Daluan stood looking thoughtfully down at the cairn, his dark head bare.

"I did," he said simply. "I would have given him a king's burying, but I was my lone."

"Mad," I thought to myself, my pulses quickening, "or he would never pretend to have buried a man of '98—a lad like him."

"The world wears on to sundown, and love is lost and won,
But he recks not of loss or gain—the King of Ireland's son—
He follows on for ever when all your chase is done—
He follows after shadows—the King of Ireland's son.

"Then he looked at me, smiling, and answered my thoughts as he had done before.

"You don't understand—quite. But the sun sets and rises outside Carlow, Sidier Rhu."

"I never said it didn't," I said, rather sharply. "What place is that over there? Do you know it?"

"I think I know every house in Ireland," he said simply, "from Derry of the oakwoods to Donegal of the strangers. That place is the 'Rood House' Inn: it was a nunnery of Bridget's long ago."

"I shall put up there for a while," I said. "And you?" He looked at me, smiling. "I shall stay with you for a while," he said. You will be sorry, perhaps, but you may be glad afterwards, Brian aroon." I was sorry, but I was not anxious to show it, so I hastily denied his assertion.

"I am very glad to have so amusing a comrade, Daluan," I said. "But why do you call me Brian? That is my second name, but I am always called by my first—Archibald."

"Brian is best," Daluan observed quietly. "Let us go in and eat: it is a long way from Kilclary." I was getting used now to his apparent knowledge of my movements, and so made no sign of surprise, but entered the long rambling coffee-room of the Rood House, and ordered dinner for two. However, I might have spared my pains, for when the meal was served Daluan would have none of the baked meats I had chosen, but broke his fast with a couple of potatoes and a draught of milk, brought in a queer horn goblet, lettered with some strange legend in Irish characters which I could not decipher. The waiter, a red-headed lad with a pair of merry blue eyes, watched us both pretty sharply, I saw, and I fancied that he drew a long breath of relief when I rose and proposed to continue our journey, not desirous of spending the night in the 'Rood House' as would be our probable fate if we waited for the heavy clouds that were rolling up from the east. "Let us go, then," Daluan said as I paid the red-haired youth: "the best of the day is gone. See the dust dancing." I drew back from the open doorway to avoid the whirling dust, but he stepped out into the midst of it, with a curious gesture—I could not tell if it were addressed to me, nor yet if it were of reproach, derision, or farewell. It may have been the latter, for when the dust-cloud left the way clear, there was no sign of Daluan in the road, or in the stony fields stretching away to the horizon-line.

"Odd," I said, surprised, "but he is odd. My change? ah, thanks! Can't you keep your mouth shut, man?" I suppose Daluan's disappearance had irritated me more than I knew, for the waiter's gaping astonishment put me almost past all self-control. "Here, there's a silver key for you," and I tossed him another shilling. "Well, what's the matter now?" "Will yir honour take it back?" the fellow almost whimpered. "'Tis fairy money, sure, and I'd have the comether put on me for touchin' ut: Och, put it away, sorr, an' get away wid ye: we never did ye anny harm, sure: Lord be betune us an avil!"

I delivered myself of some Ossianic denunciation, threw the money in his frightened face, and departed, vowing by Neptune and Nebuchadnezzar to be very careful in my choice of travelling companions next time.

The years swept along at a rate that soon obliterated chance impressions.

One day in October—the 31st, I believe—I, a Major now, and a one-armed Major at that, went to Galway to spend a few days with an old friend and some time brother-in-arms, one Felix O'Flaherty, developed by easy circumstances and a bachelor life into a dilettante antiquary. We had gone together to visit a certain rath supposed to be haunted by the ghosts of a Dé Danann King and Queen, and in the dusk I turned down the wrong path, missing O'Flaherty, who had been walking a few yards in front. I was half-way down the lane before I found out my mistake, and, hearing a sound of voices in advance, I persevered in my way. Presently, the lane widened out, and, without any warning, I came upon a mourning group of men and women assembled in a great circle round a mound that looked like a newly-turfed grave. It was the women, by the way, who formed the circle: and there was just twilight enough for me to see their faces set white in the blackness of their hooded cloaks. The men stood back in the shadows of the stone fence, but I could hear their cry well enough, and I wondered at it not a little, knowing that the keen is generally raised by women. And this was the burden of the keen, or, at least, all of it that I could understand: "Daluan is dead—dead! Daluan is dead." Then, with a burst of laughter from the women, infinitely sadder than their moaning, hitherto inarticulate, came the cry "Da Mort is King." I turned back, and made the best of my way homewards as soon as might be: and after dinner I told the story to O'Flaherty when his flow of antiquarian anecdote flagged a little, and asked him what it meant, and who was dead in the neighbourhood. "Nobody *I* know," he said, laying his pipe down "and I thought I heard all the news. Fergus," to his man who was adroitly reviving a dying fire, "who has died lately?" "Nobody, sir." "But you hear what Major Browne says." Fergus stood up and saluted, but did not take his eyes from the fire. "I heard, sir. The Major went down the Black Boreen." "And you think that explains matters?" "I do, sir. Did the Major know any of the faces?" "No: I saw no men, only heard them," I explained. "But I should know one woman in the group if I met her again: an oldish woman with red hair, and a peculiarly white face. Not ill-looking by any means and blind too, I think."

"Biddy Va'an, who died last year," master and man said with one voice. I laughed uneasily. "Do you mean to say I've been seeing ghosts, Felix?" "To-night's the 31st of October," Fergus said meaningly. "What was the name you heard, Major?" "Daluan." "You've heard it before?" O'Flaherty said quickly. "Well, it isn't an Irish name, Archie— at least nobody owns it now." "I met a fellow once with that name," I said, thinking aloud. "Only—what are you driving at, Felix?"

"Oh-h, nothing: Only Da Luan is Irish for Monday. I thought it might have struck you before, old fellow."

"It didn't. And now, Felix?"

"Well, you said the keen ended with, 'Monday is dead: Tuesday is King.' My dear fellow, rub up your memory a little. Did you never read of Greek dryads and fauns shrieking 'Pan is dead: great Pan is dead.' Yes: of course you have. Well, Keltic fairies were said to vary their lament thus: 'Monday is dead.'"

"And you mean to say—my dear Felix, it's preposterous—" I broke off angrily. " In these material days no one would believe.—You were joking?"

"Was I? We'll go to the Black Boreen to-morrow, Archie, and if we get light or sight of Da Luan's grave I'll eat my words, and my hat too. Man alive, there are pishogues and sheogues in Ireland yet, for all the mills in Belfast and Armagh."

We did go to the Black Boreen next day, but we found level turf instead of a mound, and over the place where I thought I had seen the newly-turned sods there was growing a patch of bogcotton and ragweed.

Una of the West.

Una of the West.

It's "Una, Una, Una!"
The birds cry after me,
When I go back at sunset
Into my own country—
With "Una, Una, Una,"
They will not let me be.

With Druid leaves they crowned me
The mistress of the Shee,
East wind and west they gave me,
For hounds to follow me:
Mine are the yellow ragweeds
And mine the quicken tree.

I teach the dreaming colleen
How she her love may win:
I wake old harps from silence
To wail for days of Fionn:
I make the long grass greener
That folds Saint Idé in.

It's "Una, Una, Una,"
Birds sing and will not stay:
And not a plover whistles
Or lark dare greet the day
Until I come from westward
And bid the night away.

The Soul of Maurice Dwyer.

THE SOUL OF MAURICE DWYER.

"There is a power o' ugly things in the wood of Foynes," said the good people of St. Donart's, a little village in an out-of-the-way corner of Munster, and so Maurice Dwyer said to himself as he paused under a blackened birch-tree in this same wood, looking and listening with such a cold fear tugging at his heart-strings as he had never felt before in all his sixteen years.

"Is there anny one there?" he cried, as the under-growth shook and stirred. "If there is, let him spake, for the love of Mary."

"For the love of Mary I'll do naught," said a tall man, clad from head to foot in dull gray, as he bent the reeds and grasses to right and left, and stepped out into the clearer footpath. "What would you have of me, boy? Speak out: and don't stand trembling like a rabbit."

"I've no cause to tremble," Maurice Dwyer

said, quietly, "I want to know are ye the Great Dhoul himself, or only a shlip o' the same stock?"

"Civilly now, my boy," the man in gray said, placidly. "No, I am not the Great Dhoul —say I am only one of his servants. Why do *you* come here, Maurice Dwyer? It's your mother I and my master have to do with."

"Sure it is," Maurice said, "and she's in mortal terror for her soul, lest ye'd have power upon it, since she's taken up with Phaudrig Gorey, and him with a vanithee of his own in County Antrim."

"Mortal terror she may well be in, if she holds her soul dear, for 'tis nearly ours, and a poor slip of a soul it is, after all our trouble: and the sins of it scarcely worth a thraneen."

"Then let it go," Maurice pleaded. "Sure, she loves Phaudrig well: and the woman in Antrim's an idle stravag as ever was. Let my mother's soul go free."

"Softly, now: the Great Dhoul does nothing for nothing, Maurice. What have you got to offer for Mauryeen Dwyer's soul?"

"There's my own."

"Your own soul, is it? Well, it may be worth more to my Master than your mother's."

"Take it, then," Maurice said, drawing a deep breath. "Sure, she has been a kind mother to me: and I'll burn for her, with a heart and a half."

"Will you?" said the man in gray, smiling. Take a minute to choose—the Dhoul is a fair dealer." As he spoke, Maurice Dwyer reeled back against the scorched tree-trunk, panting, caught in the grip of an agony crueller than death.

"Well?" said the man in gray. "You may cry to Mary and all the saints, but it will never cease. And if you call in priest and doctor, neither can help you. Be at peace now." He lifted his hand, and the fiery pain was gone, leaving the boy still panting and trembling with the memory of it. "Now choose. Her pain or yours?"

"My pain!" the boy said, faintly but steadily: and the man in gray laughed maliciously, as he signed him on breast and brow. "Now burn," he said, "as you have chosen, fool. And here, that you may not blab of this night's doing, for our Master loves silent subjects——" He stooped and kissed Maurice full on the lips. "Love and hate, court and marry, help and destroy henceforward as you will, but be dumb, in the name of the Dhoul. If your tongue desires freedom, it shall be free to speak the great Dhoul's name. And now, farewell—or fare ill, I care not."

"Maurice? Maurice agra, what are you doing here deep in the wood? There are wicked things here, my mother says."

Mairgread's soft cheek was pressed to his, and Mairgread's fingers pulled his hand away from his eyes.

"Maurice avick, what is it ails you? Why don't you speak to me? Or," flushing and drawing sharply back, "have you taken the rue?" Maurice shook his head, struggling desperately to speak and break the charm, but his tongue failed him in his need, and he could only stand and look at the girl with loving, hopeless eyes.

"Is it a pishogue that's been put on you?" Mairgread asked, suddenly. "Sure, you had your speech this morning: or is it a trick you're playing me, Maurice Dhu?" Maurice shook his head again: and Mairgread's puzzled face grew suddenly scared and white.

"Is it worse than a pishogue? Is it devilment?" she gasped. "Augh, and the ill name that the wood's got! In the name of Mary, answer me, Maurice Dwyer—have the ill things got hold upon ye?" It was better to end the little tragedy at once: Maurice nodded. Mairgread drew back a step or two, looking fixedly at his downcast face: then as he raised his head, and looked her squarely in the eyes she turned with a faint cry, and plunged into the bushes, sobbing as she went. Maurice set his teeth and turned his face homewards. The next time he set eyes on Mairgread Rua, he was a man grown, and she was foremost among a band of women who had lain in wait for him on the lonely Derrycarn road, to stone him as he trudged along the way to the wretched hut that sheltered him. Mairgread's aim was surer than that of the other women, and her missiles came so swiftly that Maurice's forehead and cheek were soon cut and bleeding. " Augh, let me go," Mairgread cried, suddenly, throwing up her arm to cover her eyes, " 'tis the evil eye that he's looking at me wid. Let me go, Maurice Dwyer: turn your eyes away, they're dhrawin' me heart out ov me body."

Maurice turned away, with a smile on his lips, and went quietly on his homeward way, The door of his hut stood wide open, and over the open fireplace stood a tall man, holding his hands over the burning turfs. As Maurice's shadow fell at his feet he turned with a start, and Maurice Dwyer saw the face of the man in gray. " You ? " said his uninvited guest. " *You*, Dwyer? I asked after you, and the fools here said you were dead. How has the world used you, man? I played a sorry trick upon you when I saw you last. Why don't you speak?" With sudden irritation. "Good God!—recoiling a step—"do you mean to say you never found me out?"

Maurice shook his head. The other made a hasty movement with his open hands, and then Maurice opened his lips and spoke, in a strange halting voice. "Was it all a thrick, thin? and you no dhoul at all? Wirrasthrue, and was it for this that my mother died and wouldn't spake to me? And the days black to me, and the ways sore, by rason of your thrick!" "Say what you please," the man said humbly. "It was a cruel trick, but if I had known how it was to hurt you—"

"Who are ye, at all?" Maurice Dwyer said. "And what did ye know of me, and mine? And how comes it that the pain tuk me at your bidding, man alive?"

"That was pure chance. I am a Limerick man, and the world had gone wrong with me, and I was ready for any mischief. And then I had heard in Foynes of your mother, and how her man was no husband: and the woman that told me this said too that you had gone to the wood to make terms with the Dhoul—curse the meddling tongue of her!" "Let curses be! Maybe her tongue's still to-day," Maurice said hoarsely. "Well, 'tis over, sure, and I bear ye no malice—though ye put a load on my back that came nigh to breaking it. But what's done's done: and there are no hearts broken over it.—Hould me back, jewel—" suddenly grasping the stranger's arm with both hands, "if ye're not the Dhoul indeed, for there's a black pit at my feet, and—"

"For God's sake, speak to me," said the man from Limerick, as Maurice's head fell back against his breast. "There's surely a Dhoul— if there's a God at all, speak, man, and say you forgive me."

"There *is* a God," Maurice said. "And I bid Him bless ye—"

Perhaps He would, in days to come: but before the stranger could answer, He had taken the soul of Maurice Dwyer to Himself, and Sheeoge nor Dhoul had further power upon it. to bless—or to ban.

Kasár of the Fomoroh.

Kasár of the Fomoroh.

Deathsmitten by the light of the Dé Danann
      Thou wert, Kasár:
Their glory grows and deepens but not wholly
      Outshines thy star.

Thy star is pale and shines thro' dark clouds drifting;
      The east wind cold
Blows on it: yet it darkens not, but quenches
      Dé Danann gold.

O light of many tribes that dwelt in darkness,
      Fierce and forlorn:
First star to light the hunters in the stormy
      Fomorian morn.

First star beloved of men, first star forgotten,
      O morning star—
Be near me, dusk or dawning—lead me sunwards,
      Kasár, Kasár!

The Gifts of Aodh and Una.

THE GIFTS OF AODH AND UNA.

"WHEN will the plague cease?" the people of Brefny cried. "When will the curse be lifted from our homes, and the blight from our fields? Answer us this: O ye Ollavs." And the Ollavs said in answer: "Hearken in patience a little, O men and women of Brefny. Surely ye shall be free from the plague, and surely the famine shall be ended, when a maid and boy of royal blood deliver themselves over, body and soul, to the ancient gods whom ye have deserted, in the temples ye have dishonoured." The Princes of O'Rourke, Adamnan, Fergus and Aodh, looked at each other, and drew quickly away from the little crowd of nobles and Brehons round the carved golden chair where old King Eochaidh sat to give justice to his people—"in the eye of the sun."

"Didst thou hear, brother?" Fergus the soldier said to Adamnan the scholar. "The gods have spoken—not the new gods that our mother worships—but the old gods of our fathers: and they will not be denied. Who is to go? I am aptest at swordplay, but what is swordplay against ghosts?" "I have married a wife," Adamnan said calmly, "and I cannot go. Aodh, is thy heart high enough for this?" Aodh smiled: and a spot of colour came into Adamnan's pale face as he met his young brother's grave eyes. "Thou wilt do it?" he said, "Ghosts and all, young Aodh? Bethink they will have thee body and soul." Aodh turned and looked down at the clustering huts below the hill where they stood. "The blue mist still steams up and slays my father's people," he said gravely. "Let us go to my father, brothers: for his heart is sore till the plague be stayed amid his people."

"It is not fair for thee to bide the trial, our youngest," Fergus protested. "I will rather go, and if the worst come to the worst—well, do thou comfort Brighid."

"Nay, good my brother," Aodh said gently. "Adamnan has his wife Eiver, and thou art troth-plight to Brighid: therefore it is fittest for me to go, who have no love and no lady."

"It *is* fittest for thee to go, my brother," Adamnan said, with a sudden flush on his face.

"For surely thou hast the bravest heart of us three, and the whitest soul. And so may our mother's gods shield thee, Aodh, and our own gods deal gently with thee —"

"Let them deal with me as they will," Aodh said, as he turned once more to look down at the clustered huts in the valley, "so they spare my father's people. Let us to my father now—and wilt thou speak for me, Adamnan, and declare my purpose? My tongue is not as ready as thine." Adamnan put his arm round his young brother's shoulders, and the three went slowly back to the little crowd of nobles, Brehons, and priests surrounding the King's chair, and looking down in troubled silence at the clamouring, famine-stricken crowd below them. The nobles gave back to let the princes pass, and Aodh went quickly up to his father, and knelt there, Adamnan standing over him, with a caressing hand laid on his dark hair.

"Father," Adamnan said, raising his voice a little. "Father—and my people—the man has been found that will give his soul and his body to the ancient gods, that they may spare thy people and thy fields of yellow corn."

"He has been found?" King Eochaidh said quaveringly. "Not thou—not thou, O my son Adamnan?"

"Nay, my liege: not I," Adamnan said gravely. "Neither I nor Fergus: but he that will give these gifts kneels here."

"Aodh? Our little Aodh?" the Princess Eiver cried incredulously, as she sprang up from her seat on the short green grass. Adamnan lifted his head and looked at his wife with something like anger in his black eyes. "O Lady of Brefny, not so," he answered sharply. "Henceforward my brother shall be called of us 'Little Aodh' no longer: but Aodh Great-Heart."

"Rise, my son—" Eochaidh said, leaning forward, "and answer for thyself, in the eye of the sun. Is this thy will indeed, to give this gift of thyself to thy father, and thy father's people?"

"It is my will, indeed, my lord and my father," Aodh said, facing round to the people for a moment, as he stood up, "I give the gift with all my heart, to thee and to my people."

"We accept the gift, Prince Aodh," his father said solemnly. "Lean thou hither that I may kiss thee—the last of my kisses, little Aodh.—And now," as he stood up and laid two trembling hands on Aodh's shoulders, "hither, ye priests of Crom and of Aongus, and take this gift of Prince Aodh. Farewell, son; henceforward thou art the gods'—not mine.

Farewell." "Farewell," Aodh said smiling, as the priests came eagerly about him. " Now, fathers, I am yours: and what geasa do ye lay upon me?"

"None yet," said the eldest priest, Miledh, "but fast ye must, and pray ye must, and make pure your flesh with the water of the Breed well: and ye must put on the saffron and scarlet of a King's son: and afterwards we will give ye to the gods. But hark ye, brothers: here is the boy, but where is the maid? Is there no daughter of the royal house will give a royal gift to her people—like this Aodh?" He spoke to the King: but the King lay back in his seat with both wrinkled hands covering his face, and for a space there was no answer. Then, as Miledh's eyes travelled round the circle of nobles and Brehons, there stepped forth from it the Princess Eiver, splendid in her trailing robes of blue and saffron, with a diamond blazing in the fillet round her forehead: and she said: "I have a little sister, of the royal blood of Ullad: and pure she is as the first snow, and fair enow for a gift to the gods: and for a year and a day she has dwelt among my handmaidens, and neither has she loved, nor been loved. Bide ye here a little while I send for her. Maiden Moirin, go hence swiftly and call the lady Una from her spinning: and," in a low voice, "say only to her that her sister desires her presence." There was a silence: and the pebbles of the hillside were scattered by hurrying girlish feet, and Aodh saw the Princess Una for the first time: for hitherto she had sat unseen among her sister's many maidens. She was little and slender and pale like a lily, and drooped her yellow head a little, like a lily : and in her dress she wore the lily's colours of white and green, and her rosy feet were bare under the garment's hem. "Daughter of Nuad," the Princess Eiver said, as the girl drew near, "and sister of my heart, it is my will that thou goest forth with these priests of great Crom, and that thou doest their will as thou hast done mine, without question, and in all things. And I lay this geasa upon thee that thou art dumb until this chief amongst them, giveth thee leave to speak. Now do my will maiden Una." The girl bent her fair head in silence, and gave her hand to Miledh and let him lead her away, with just one last backward glance at her sister, of such gentle wonder as made Aodh's heart burn within him, as he followed after her to the great golden temple of Crom. "She is a child," he said to those that walked beside him, "and she does not know. My sister Eiver has no right to give her life away : it was a cruel deed. Is there no other woman will take her place, and save the people of Brefny?"

"No other, lord."

"At least, then," Aodh pleaded, "take her not blindly to her death. Tell her what thing lies before her: she is a royal maiden, and not a sheep to be driven dumb to the slaughter."

"Have no fear, my son," a young priest said in his ear. "Miledh is my mother's brother, and I will plead with him that he lift the geasa from the maiden or ever we give ye to the gods."

Aodh sighed and fell silent: there was small use in protest, for the priests and the gods and the people were all on one side, and what was one girl's life to these? After all, it was best to endure, and be silent: and in silence he suffered them to bathe and clothe him as richly as they would, and in silence, when the two days of fasting were over, he lay in the litter they had prepared for him, and felt his bearers stumble over the scattered stones in the valley. Neither priests nor soldiers came near him then, but at the end of the first day's journey his litter was set down in a green little glen where a stream ran tinkling under slender birch trees, and the curtains of it were drawn back by Miledh himself. "Rise, and eat," he said, "and be free to speak, Prince Aodh: for the geasa is lifted from the lady Una, and her lips are loosed. I lay it upon thee, my son, to tell her whither she is journeying."

"I know to what end we journey, my father," Aodh said. " But I also know not whither."

" There are twain temples on an island in the Shannon," Miledh said, smiling, "and one is builded to the heroes of the Fianna : and one is the temple of Crom Mighty. And the maiden Una must into the shrine of the Mighty One : and there work his will."

"And I to the temple of the Fianna," Aodh said quietly. " It is well, my father : and I will tell the princess what lies before her —if the telling of the tale is laid upon me."

" In the name of Crom the Thunderer I lay it on thee, Aodh, son of Eochaidh," Miledh said sternly. " Up, daughter Una, and give greeting to this kinsman of thine." Una started up hurriedly from the fallen tree whereon she had seated herself, and moved a step or two forward, to meet Aodh. " I give thee greeting, kinsman and Prince," she said, modestly. "Art thou later from Brefny than I, and canst thou give me news of my lord the King and my sister the lady Eiver ? "

" Nay, lady Una : for I left Brefny when thou didst : and my litter has been but a few yards behind thine all day."

'I did not see thee," Una said. "Are we to be faring-fellows all the way, knowest thou?"

"All the way whither, Lady Una?"

"I do not know. My sister bade me ask no questions," Una said simply. "I may speak now — my father yonder saith — but whither we go I have not asked."

"It is full time for thee to know, my daughter," Miledh said gravely. "Speak, Prince Aodh."

"Ay, tell me," Una said innocently. "Do we go to my sister Maiga in Connaught? 'Tis a long journey and a sore."

"Nay, little princess," Aodh said very gently, "but we go farther yet. Hast thou not heard that the gods are angry, and the folk of Brefny die by scores, and the wheat is blighted?"

"Ay." Una nodded. "I have heard." "So the priests sought the gods' will, and they learned that Crom would slay and not spare until two of royal blood—a man and a maid— were given over to the angry gods to work their will—to torment and to slay as they pleased. O child," Aodh broke off suddenly, "canst thou not guess the rest?" Una gave a little cry, and shrank back. "Am I the maid chosen? Art thou the man? Oh cruel! cruel! We are too young to die."

"Nay, Princess Una!" Aodh drew the

sobbing child into his arms and held her fast. "I have seen seventeen good years, and thou how many?"

"Fifteen," sobbed Una.

"Fifteen happy years, and now a great deed has come to thy hand, and thou wilt surely do it. Is it not a great deed to bring back blood to thy people's withered veins, and give bread to their hungry mouths? And to feed and heal them we have but to die."

"But will the gods be kind," Una sobbed, "and slay us swiftly? Kinsman, I am afraid—I am afraid—Thou wilt stand by me."

"Nay now, king's daughter, be of stronger heart," Aodh said gravely. "I go alone to the temple of the Fianna, and thou alone to the shrine of Crom, and there we submit our bodies and our souls to the gods to do with as they will. And the ghosts of our fathers will be with us to watch that we shame them not in any torment. Art thou still afraid, O Princess?"

"Not with such deadly fear," Una whispered, "but the shrine will be dark and cold and dreadful—and I shall surely shriek and shame my fathers—"

"Nay: thou wilt suffer all nobly, and shriek not at all," Aodh said tenderly. "Thou wilt know I shall be listening from the midmost of mine own ordeal—and—There, kinswoman," as Una drew herself away from his clasp, with a proud flush on her face, "so should a lady of Eri look, when she goes to an unknown terror for love's sake."

"For love's sake?" Una's large blue eyes were brightened with a new and strange light. "For love's sake shall I yield me into Crom's hands, Prince Aodh?" Aodh put out his hands hurriedly to her and his eyes took fire from hers.

"For love's sake only, Una of Ullad, and for no other in the world." He drew her to him and kissed her on the forehead, and presently on the lips: and then the priest Miledh spoke, smiling his strange mocking smile meanwhile. "Ye have taken your food from the gods' table," he said, "and now ye must eat of our earthly food, lady and lord. Here are cresses from the brook, and a woman has come hither with new-baked cakes in her veil, and a noggin of new milk: so here will we sit and break bread together, for I also am royal, and of the clan Orgiall."

"I also am royal," Aodh said smiling too, "but my royalty will serve thine age, father—and my lady's womanhood." He moved away a few steps and came back with the jar of milk and the smoking cakes wrapped in fresh green leaves. "Drink, father; for the way was long and dusty to-day—And drink thou too, dear heart."

"I drink to thee, my Prince," Una said as she finished her draught; and broke a cake with him. Miledh laughed.

"'Tis a pretty play," he said, "and 'tis good to be young and lovers, yet forget not what stands back of all this, Prince and Princess. No marriage-vows and marriage bed for ye: only a kiss or two stolen before ye kiss Death."

"I had forgotten," Una said faintly. "Ay, he is right, Aodh, and we will kiss no more. Death is stronger than we are."

"Nay: that he is not, for we have come so far to seek him of our own free will, sweet Una. Kiss again we will—ay, and even when the doors of Death stand open for us."

"Brave words, my son: and 'tis wisdom to be merry when going to grip with Messer Death. And not a kiss will I balk ye of," Miledh said, with his strange smile, "but my task it shall be to remember ye midmost of your kisses of the terror to come."

"I drink to thee, my Princess," Aodh said, with a touch on Una's folded hands.

"Drink: as once I drank to a fairer lady," Miledh said. "But my kisses turned to ashes on my lips when my bride turned from her sage to a mere soldier, and spent on him her heart's gold with small return : and for the sake of my spoiled kisses I am blithe to-night, young lovers, to bid ye kiss and kiss, and remember those that wait for thee, Princess, in the temple of Crom—and those that will make merry with thy pains, Prince, in the House of the Heroes." Aodh laughed as Una stood up, and put her hand trustfully in his.

"Let us wait until the House of the Heroes is in our sight," he said. "Sweet, shall I put thee in thy litter, or wilt thou walk afoot? It cannot be far hence to the river-edge."

"It is not far," Miledh said. "Nor also is it far to the Houses of Crom and the Heroes." It was not far : for the oarsmen had not rowed the boats down the clear waters of the Shannon for more than an hour, when a shadowy island hove in sight, and in a few minutes the travellers were standing knee-deep in the tall grass, shading their eyes against the westering sun, as it dropped down in gold and scarlet behind the black ruin of Crom's temple.

"We are here at our journey's end," Miledh said, as the little company paused with one consent. "Yonder is the place beloved of Crom, and—look eastward—there shines the House of the Heroes." It shone indeed in the face of the sunset, its great pillars wreathed round with fantastic carved shapes of god and devil, its great door glistering with plates of gold: and on its roof a huge hound crouched as if for a spring, and the rains had worn seams down its stone sides.

"We are here," Miledh repeated. "Daughter, thine hour has come." Una went forward a step or two, then drew back with a cry of terror as the door of Crom's temple swung open and closed again.

"Aodh, help!"

"There is no help in Aodh," Miledh said. "Come, daughter of a king, and be of good heart: thy kinsman goeth to the same fate." Una looked round hurriedly: Aodh was already on the moss-grown steps of the temple of the Fianna, and the sunset blazed on his face as he turned round to the watchers, showing it as quiet as it had been when Una saw him first, in the valley of the cresses. He waved his hand to her in mute greeting and farewell, and set his hands against the gilded door, which was slow to yield—so slow that, still pushing, he turned his head and saw Una's white garments fluttering in the wind as she put her soft palms against the temple-door and pushed it slowly back—saw the love and fear striving together in her face—and heard the cry she gave as the darkness swallowed her up. Then the door at which he was striving opened wide, and from the dark shrine swept out a cloud of fine grey dust. The door clanged to behind him, and he went up the aisle walking ankle-deep in the fine dust, and straining his eyes to see through the darkness if indeed figures paced beside him, and ghostly groups gave way before him, as he could not help but fancy. At last his outstretched hands touched a twisted horn of some smooth cold substance, and he knew that he had reached the end of his journey. With his left hand clinging to the horn he turned towards the dark temple, saying aloud, "Here I stand, Aodh, with gifts to give the Fianna and their gods. In the name of my mother's God, let them who desire my gifts, come to me." "Aodh, son of Eochaidh," a shivering voice cried out, "give me thy youth." "I give," Aodh said quietly. "Aodh!" said another voice, reedy and thin but sweet, "give me thy knowledge: I, Grania, loved much and knew little." There was a gray figure at his side, and without a word Aodh turned and laid his forehead on the ghost's cold breast. As he rested thus, another voice said, "I am Oisin: give me thy death, O Aodh!" Aodh drew a deep breath, then he lifted his head, and clasped a ghostly figure in his arms, and holding it there, felt it stiffen and grow rigid and colder yet. "Give me thine hope, Aodh!" "Give me thy faith, Aodh!" "Give me thy courage, Aodh!" "Give me thy dreams, Aodh!" So the voices called and cried, and to each Aodh answered, and gave the desired gift. "Give me thine heart, Aodh," cried another. "I am Maive, who knew much and loved little." And with a sickening sense of pain Aodh felt slender cold fingers scratching and tearing their way through flesh and sinew till they grasped his heart, and tore the fluttering thing away. "Give me thy love, Aodh!" another implored. "I am Angus, Master of Love, and I have loved none."

"Take it," Aodh said faintly: and there was a pause. But soon the shivering voices began again, and the cold fingers clutched at his bare arms and feet, and the breath of ghostly lips played on his cheek as the cloudy figures came and went, and struggled and scrambled about him, until they all fell silent and still at the tread of mighty feet up the dark church. "Son of a King," said a voice, deep and clear and full. "Aodh, what hast thou left to give to me —Fionn?" "I have nothing left to give my King," Aodh said wearily. "I have given all I have, except my soul." "It is that I desire," said the mighty voice. Aodh hesitated for a moment, and then he stretched out his hands.

"Take it, if it is mine to give, O King: and now let me die."

"Didst thou not give thy death to my son Oisin but now?"

"I remember," Aodh said faintly. "I will live then, God pity me!"

"Wilt thou have thy gifts again, Prince Aodh?"

"Nay, what man gives and takes again?" Aodh said still more faintly—"what I gave I gave—" He had an instant's glimpse of a noble face smiling down at him, then the fine gray dust was in his eyes and ears, blinding and deafening him, and the next moment he was standing out in the free air once more. He drew in a long breath of the salt sharp wind, and lifting his dazed eyes for a moment, looked round and saw Una lying at his feet in her purple litter, white and still and beautiful, with her hands crossed meekly on her breast, and a look of defiance frozen on her face. Miledh put his arms hurriedly about the young man, but Aodh kept himself closely in check, and the face he bent down to Una's, when he kissed her, was set as sternly as her own. Then he rose up and went down through the long grass, Miledh keeping step with him: nor was his utter stillness broken when they laid Una on the deck on a bed of purple, and the old priest broke down into unwilling tears to hear the rowers chanting softly of " Una bawn " and her goodness and her graces.

"Art thou dumb, boy?" Miledh cried, at last, "or didst thou find a fairer mistress in yonder dark temple?"

"I found no other mistress," Aodh said. "And wherefore should I speak, when I cannot heal?"

"She gave a great gift," Miledh said, "and her memory will be blessed for ages to come. What didst thou give, O Aodh, besides thy youth? Thy head is as white as mine."

"What matter?" Aodh said, wearily. "She gave: and I gave; and who shall reckon up our gifts?"

"Ay indeed, what matter?" Miledh assented. "Lie down and sleep, my son, and gather strength for the burdens of to-morrow." Aodh shook his head hopelessly, but the kind sleep came whether he would or no, and Miledh slept too, and soundly, with his head resting on the foot of Una's couch.

The next day, and the next, the rowers were forbidden by Aodh to keen for Una, but the priests took harp and tympan, and striking these they brought Una with royal music up the untrodden pathway of the river, and with the same music carried her up the hill side and laid her at her sister's feet in the high hall of Brefny. Then there was wailing of women, and hurried speech among the men, but over all the clamour rose high the music of the priests, and the voice of Aodh singing the bridal song of Una of Ullad. And when it was done, he fell as a stricken tree falls, and Adamnan caught him in his arms, and carried him away to his chamber: and there for many days he tended him with wizard charms and incantations. But always he lay as one that is dead, but for the light in his eyes and the speech of his lips, and when the Prince felt his heart to see if it beat, lo, it beat not at all: so the Lady Eiver cried out that it was a devil dwelling in the dead body of Aodh, and she fled from the chamber, and would not look upon him again. And when Fergus would speak with him of old battles, there was no memory in him, and no knowledge: and when Brighid, the wife of Fergus, wept over him for the sake of childish days when they had played together, he put her from him, smiling, and said a word that only Adamnan could understand—how he had given youth and love away. And always he went encompassed with dreams, even when he stood beside his father in the forefront of the battle, and saw Fergus fall, with an arrow in his heart: and when Adamnan died, being full of days, and the people came to crown him, the dreams held him still.

When seventy years had passed, and he wore a boy's face still under his gray hair, he called about him the wisest Ollavs and bade them try their spells to release him from his weary body, and set him free to sleep beside Una of Ullad. But their spells and charms were useless: so once more Aodh took boat down the Shannon, and once more thrust open the gilded door of the Heroes' House. And if he died there, and found Una of Ullad, or if he lives there still I do not know: but the people of Brefny still speak of a noble gift as the "gift of Una," though of the greater gifts of Aodh they do not speak. But in the House of the Heroes the gifts are remembered every one: and the name of Aodh is honoured as is the name of Diarmuid.

Lament of the Lay Brother.

Lament of the Lay Brother.

(A.D. 598.)

Iona, O Iona,
   My days go sad and slow,
For mid your island meadows
   I hear no cattle low.
I miss the fields of Kerry,
   The green fields and the kine,
And in my brothers' chanting
   Is heard no voice of mine—
      Iona, O Iona!

Iona, O Iona,
   My mates are glad of cheer,
But I, the Kerry peasant,
   Dwell sad and lonely here.
I send an exile's sighing
   Across the sundering sea;
O would I were in Kerry,
   Or the kine were here with me!

Iona, O Iona,
  The Saint sleeps well, I trow,
Nor dreams that one poor brother's
  Heartbroke for Ireland now—
Heartbroke to be a herd-boy
  And watch the cattle feed,
And call the cattle homewards
  Across the darkening mead.

Iona, O Iona,
  All summer swallows stay
About your towers: the seagulls
  To Ireland take their way.
And would, I cry with weeping,
  The seagulls' road were mine—
To hear and see the lowing,
  The kind eyes of the kine!
    Iona, O Iona!

The Four Kings.

THE FOUR KINGS.

"THERE is a curse upon us," the men of Glandore whispered among themselves, as they stood watching the sun go redly to his setting one Friday evening some centuries ago. "There's a curse upon us, sure, for haven't we crowned a new king every season this year? Earrach was in its last month when we were bringing out our skenes for King Brian; then comes the fever, and King Rory stands up with his foot on his brother's grave. Rory was King all Samhradh, and when Foghmhar came to us we were kingless, and the hand of the Queen was heavy on us till we chose Brian's child our lord. And now Geimhridh is on us: and the child Feargus is lost, and heavier on us than the Queen's hand is the hand of the Queen's new mate, Oscur of Glandore. And to-night is King Oscur sick to death, and we shall surely hear Cleena's wave boom out yonder in the harbour: for evil though Oscur be, he is King in Glandore, and Cleena's wave sounds always for the death of a king in Erin." But the women whispered a different story, as they sat spinning over the peat-fires: and their tongues lashed only the name of the Queen, Maive, and softly they spoke of the King who lay a-dying, for he had borne a comely face and a gracious presence, and he had been lavish both of gold and gentle speeches, wherefore they forgot the dreamer King Brian, and the soldier Rory, and the kidnapped Feargus had no place in their thoughts. One only thought of him and cursed Fair Oscur: and she sat, laying on him evil wishes, and praying not to Christ or Mary, but to the Dada Mor and to Lug that the ghosts of Brian and Brian's child, and Rory the Fighter might stand by his bedside, and whisper his black deeds over one by one. As she sat, thus, her daughter sat near her, spinning, busy with thoughts and prayers of her own, as kind and innocent as her mother's were dark and desperate. And as she spun she sang a song which the Queen had made in the days when she was King Brian's new-wed wife, and had never seen Fair Oscur's ill-omened beauty.

> "I took to me the Flower of Sorrow,
>   Half-Summer, World's-delight :
> I snatched crushed poppies from the furrow,
>   And kissed their red to white.
> I bound the Dew-Thief* with the Mallow,
>   And Goldilocks with Rue :
> And thro' deep glens and waters shallow
>   I follow after you."

"Stop singing, colleen dhas," said the mother, after a little space. "And go you to the door, for there's a hand knocking at it."

"Mother alanna!" the girl cried, letting her wheel run slower, "it is Friday night : and this is a gentle place."

"Go to the door, and let in whoever knocks," said the mother angrily, and Maurya obeyed. She let down the bar and lifted the latch, with her heart in her mouth : then, as she saw the figure standing outside in the windy twilight, her fear died down, for there was nothing alarming in the gentle deprecating face that met hers.

"I have come far to-night," the visitor said softly, "and the wind was against me all the way. May I come in and rest beside your fire, Vanitha?" Maurya glanced at her mother, but she gave neither word nor sign in answer : and so the girl answered, doubtfully,

* Sundew.

"Come in : and the Vanitha will make you kindly welcome when she breaks her dream. Come in, and sit by the fire." She filled a cup with milk, and chose out the best of their scanty stock of potatoes for the stranger's platter : and then, having watched him eat and drink, she went back to her spinning and her song, but somehow both had changed, though not to her ears or eyes. Yet to her mother's brooding gaze the thread beside her girl's stool was of the finest, and shone like white silver, while instead of the Queen's song she chanted strange words to a tune that was infinitely old —older than the wild people of the Fomoroh. "Spindrift and Foam," she sang :

"And the wind and the sail new-wedded, and the frost on a ringing strand,
"And the sea-spirits staying us, spurring us, and the wood spirits calling us a-land,
"We returned, we returned, and were not welcome : we went forth again with empty heart and hand :
"We returned and found our cars by strangers driven, we returned and found our ships by aliens manned,
"We returned to the spindrift and the foam, my grief! and again shall we return to the land—"

"Who sang that song last?" asked the guest, as he stooped over the peat-fire : and the wise woman said, softly and unwillingly, "Kasár, lady of the Fomoroh, whom the strength of the Dé Danann slew. And better had the song slept with her." "How know you that, Vanitha?" But the mother did not answer; but listened brooding while her daughter sang on, knowing not what she sang: and over the burning peats the guest bent, holding out thin white hands to the warmth, and staring at the smoke with dreamy eyes. And Maurya sang on her burden of the "Spindrift and Foam" verse after verse, till she dropped into a lower key at the seventh verse. And now there was knocking again at the door: but now it was opened from without, and a tall man came in, shaking the rain from his mantle.

"Wild weather, Mother:" he said, "wild weather for house-keepers and worse for travellers. How wears the world with you since we met?"

"Ill enough, Rory Oge," said the wise woman, as she put her own stool near the fire for the newcomer, "and well enough, belike. Will you drink or eat?"

"Not I, Mother: there is work to do."

"I saw it a-doing in my dreams, Rory Oge."

"You were ever a dreamer, Mother: but your dreams all came true." Rory Oge stood up and threw off his cloak, and Maurya saw that he had a child in his arms, a delicate pretty boy with elfish black eyes, whose face she thought she knew.

"There," he said, as he unclasped the little hands from about his neck, "a king must stand alone. And now there is no more help in me for you, little heart." The quiet figure stooping over the fire lifted his face now, and there was in the gentle eyes a light that made Maurya's heart-strings tighten as the ghost of King Brian held out eager arms to his living child. The boy's black eyes dilated, and caught some of the light in his father's, and the two clung together for a long minute. Then King Brian lifted his head, and saw the look of pity in King Rory's brown face. "The way will be light back to Tir na n'Og to-night," he said. "I could even forgive Fair Oscur now."

"Forgive him if you will, my brother," Rory Oge said very gently. "But we must go back to Tir na n'Og alone."

King Brian's arms tightened round the boy: but he did not speak for a moment. Then he said doubtfully, "Is he not beyond all care, even as we are?"

"Look on the ground, and see," said Rory Oge. And his brother looked and saw, and bowed his head dumbly: for their two figures cast no darkness on the wooden floor, but the shadow of little King Feargus lay black at his feet.

Then the door opened wide once more: and the last guest came in—a tall slender youth wearing the "gentle" colour, green, and with a torque of twisted gold about his neck: and at sight of this gallant figure the wise woman shrieked out a curse, but Maurya fell a-sobbing, for she knew now that Oscur the Fair was dead, and that this was but his ghost come to meet the souls of the twain who had died by him. "Look at him," screamed the Vanitha. "Dada Mor and Lug Lamfada! wither him with living, and curse him with eternal life! Let him be wandering betwixt fire and frost when the gentle folk have locked themselves within the gates of Tir na n'Og."

"We have no will to punish thee:" the Kings said together, as Oscur the Fair made them a mocking salute, "though ours it was to bear the wrong. But we are the hands of the Gentle People, O Oscur, and their voice speaks for to-night through the lips of yonder woman. Be eternal life thy punishment." For a moment Oscur's gay and gallant bearing failed him, and Maurya hid her eyes from the anguish that aged and altered his beautiful face: and then she looked up once more as his answer rang boldly out. "I have planted flints on my road for myself, and I will walk on them an I must. Is your sentence finished, O ye my judges?"

"Ask the woman yonder," Rory Oge said curtly: and the Vanitha cried out, "Sharp shall the flints be, O Oscur, and sore to thy feet: and yet sorer shall it be to thee to know that feet walk and bleed beside thine—feet of one whom thou dost love. And this is the judgment of Them that sit in the golden houses of Sidh Femin and Sidh Meadha."

"But —" Oscur said, looking at her with a half-smile on his lips, "I love no one, Vanitha: and this I swear by Her who sits in a golden house at Carrig Cleena, and whose voice I heard to-night as—as I died. I must walk the flints alone, Vanitha: and even the Shee cannot put love into my heart now I am dead."

"Didst thou love no woman ere death touched thee, Oscur the Fair?" Rory Oge said quickly. "Truly, then, thou hast missed much delight."

"I have sung many serca (love-songs)" Oscur answered, "But I have loved no woman, and for this one gift held back I thank whatever gods may be. It is easier for a man to walk the flints alone."

"Art sure that thou didst love no woman?" the Vanitha asked, speaking as if the words were forced from her lips against her will.

"Look on my daughter's face, Oscur of Glandore, and call to mind a day when she crossed thy hunting-path, and found thee hurt, giving thee to drink of the new milk."

Maurya came forward a step or two, her face pale as death—paler than Oscur of Glandore's.

"Does my lord remember?" she said. "For that one day my name was 'Creevin Cno' (Cluster of nuts!)" Oscur of Glandore looked steadily at her for a moment or two: then he turned deliberately to the mother. "I do not remember, Vanitha," he said coldly: and Maurya flashed a swift look at him from eyes half-drowned with tears. "It is no use, my lord," she whispered. "The Shee saw and heard, that day: and if I were good to kiss and praise that day, I am good to follow my lord over the flints to-night."

"Is it indeed no use?" Oscur said, softly. "Must you go a-wandering, Creevin Cno, because one day in my life I saw your white soul clearly?"

"Yes: and ask no better," Maurya said passionately. "Lord, let us go: I cannot stand by and hear these judge you who do not know."

"They know me better than you, belike, white heart," Oscur said, still softly. "Is it your will to come, Creevin Cno? Remember that 'tis the mating of flesh and shadow."

"I know," Maurya murmured, "but if the flesh love the shadow—"

The door swung open and the night swallowed them up.

Lament of the Last Leprechaun.

Y

Lament of the Last Leprechaun.

For the red shoon of the Shee,
For the falling o' the leaf,
For the wind among the reeds,
    My grief!

For the sorrow of the sea,
For the song's unquickened seeds,
For the sleeping of the Shee,
    My grief!

For dishonoured whitethorn-tree,
For the runes that no man reads,
Where the gray stones face the sea,
    My grief!

Lissakeole, that used to be
Filled with music night and noon,
For their ancient revelry,
    My grief!

For the empty fairy shoon,
Hollow rath and yellow leaf;
Hands unkissed to sun or moon:
    My grief— my grief!

Aonan-na-Righ.

AONAN-NA-RIGH.

AONAN-NA-RIGH they called him in Tir Ailella*—
"Darling of the King"—but it was in idle
sport, for Cathal the Red hated the son of his
old age as men now have forgotten to hate;
and once Aonan had sprung from his sleep
with a sharp skene thrust through his arm, that
had meant to drink his life-blood; and once
again he had found himself alone in the heart
of the battle, and he had scarcely won out of
the press with his life—and with the standard
of the Danish enemy. Thus it was seen that
neither did the Danish spears love the "King's
Darling"; and the sennachies made a song of
this, and it was chanted before the King for
the first time when he sat robed and crowned
for the Beltane feast, and Aonan stood at his left
hand, pouring out honey-wine into his father's
cup. And before he drank, Cathal the King

* Now Tirerrill, Co. Sligo.

stared hard at the cup-bearer, and the red light that burned in his eyes was darkened because of the likeness in Aonan's face to his mother Acaill (dead and buried long since), whom Cathal had loved better than his first wife Eiver, who was a king's daughter, and better than the Danish slave Astrild, who bore him five sons, elder and better-loved than Aonan, for all the base blood in their veins. Of these, two were dead in the battle that had spared Aonan, and there were left to Cathal the King only the Druid Coloman, Toran the boaster, and Guthbinn of the sweet voice, who as yet was too young to fight.

"Drink, Aonan-na-Righ," shrilled Astrild from her seat at the King's left hand. "Drink: lest there be death in the cup."

Aonan took up the golden cup, and gave her back smile for smile. "I drink," he said, "to my mother, Acaill of Orgiall."

But the King snatched the cup from his finger, and dashed it down on the board, so that the yellow mead spilled and stained Astrild's cloak; but she did not dare complain, for there was the red light in Cathal's eyes that was wont to make the boldest afraid.

"Bring me another cup," he said to one that stood near. "And now, will none of ye do honour to the toast of Aonan-na-Righ?

Bring ye also a cup for the prince; and, Guthbinn, put your harp aside."

So in silence they drank to the memory of Acaill of Orgiall, and afterwards they sought to spin together the threads of their broken mirth, but not easily, for Astrild, who was wont to be gayest, sat pale, with her hand on the knife hidden in her breast; and the King sat dumb and frowning, thinking, as Astrild knew, of dead Acaill: how he had loved and hated her, and, having slain her father and brothers, and brought her to Dunna Scaith a Golden Hostage wearing a golden chain, he had wedded her for her beauty's sake; how until her child was born she had never so much as smiled or frowned for him; and how, when her babe lay in her arms, she sent for her husband, and said: "I thank thee, Cathal, who hast set me free by means of this babe. I bless thee for this last gift of thine, who for all thine other gifts have cursed thee." And Cathal remembered how he had held babe and mother to his heart, and said: "Good to hear soft words from thy mouth at last, O Acaill! Speak again to me, and softly." But she had not answered, for her first soft words to him were her last. Astrild, watching him, saw his face grow black and angry, and she smiled softly to herself, and aloud she said:

"Oh, Guthbinn, sing again, and sing of thy brothers who fell to-day—sing of Oscar, the swift in battle, and Uaithne, of the dark eyes. And will my lord give leave that I, their mother, go to weep for them in my own poor house where they were born?"

"No," said Cathal. "I bought you and your tears, girl, with gold rings, from Ocaill of Connaught. Sing to me now, and keep thy tears for to-morrow." So Astrild drove back her sorrow, and began to sing, while her son Guthbinn plucked slow music from his harp-strings.

"Earrach, Samhradh, Foghmhar, and Geimhridh,
    Are over all and done:
And now the web forgets the weaver,
    And earth forgets the sun.
I sowed no seed, and pulled no blossom,
    Ate not of the green corn:
With empty hands and empty bosom,
    Behold, I stand forlorn.
Windflower I sang, and Flower o' Sorrow,
    Half-Summer, World's Delight:
I took no thought o' the coming morrow,
    No care for the coming night."

Guthbinn's hand faltered on the harpstrings, and the singer stopped swiftly: but King Cathal stayed the tears in her heart with an angry word. "Have I not always had my will? And it is not my will now for you to weep." So

Astrild sat still, and she looked at her sons: but Toran was busy boasting of the white neck and blue eyes of the new slave-girl he had won; Coloman was dreaming, as he sat with his eyes on the stars that showed through the open door: and only Guthbinn met her eyes and answered them, though he seemed to be busy with his harp. And presently Cathal rose up, bidding all keep their seats and finish out the feast, but Astrild and Aonan he bade follow him. And so they went into the farthest chamber of the House of Shields, which looked upon a deep ditch. Now the end of the chamber was a wall of wattles, and here there was cut a door that led out on a high bank which overlooked the ditch. The King went out upon the bank, where there was a chair placed ready for him, and Astrild sat at his knee, and Aonan-na-Righ stood a little way off. And Cathal sat still for a time, holding Astrild's hand in his, and presently he said: "Who put the death in the cup to-night, Astrild, thou or Guthbinn?" Astrild tried to draw her hand away and to rise, but he held her in her place, and asked again, "Guthbinn, or thou?" until she answered him sullenly as she knelt, "King, it was I."

"Belike, Guthbinn's hand did thy bidding," he said, in laughing fashion. "Was the death for me or for Aonan yonder, thou Red-Hair?"

And Astrild laughed as she answered, "For Aonan-na-Righ, my lord." And then she shrieked and sought to rise, for she saw death in the king's face as it bent over her.

"If thou hadst sought to slay thy master, Red-Hair, I might have forgiven thee," Cathal said; "but what had my son to do with thee, my light-o'-love?"

"Give me a day," Astrild said desperately, "and I will kill father and son, and set the light-o'-love's children on your throne, Cathal."

"I doubt it not, my wild-cat, but I will not give ye the day:" Cathal laughed. "Good courage, girl—and call thy Danish gods to aid, for there is none other to help thee, now."

"What will my lord do?" Aonan said quickly, as the Dane turned a white face and flaming eyes to him. "Wouldst kill her?"

"Ay," said Cathal the King. "But first she shall leave her beauty behind her, lest she meet thy mother in the Land of Youth, and Acaill be jealous."

"Leave her beauty and breath, lord," Aonan said, drawing nearer. "If my mother Acaill lived she would not have her slain. My king, she pleased thee once; put her from thee if she vexes thee now; but leave her life, since something thou owest her."

"She would have slain thee to-day, Aonan,

and if I have dealt ill by thee, I let no other deal thus. Yet if thou prayest me for thy life, girl, for love of Acaill I will give it thee."

And Cathal laughed, for he knew the Dane would not plead in that name. Astrild laughed too. "Spare thy breath, son of Acaill," she said scornfully. "To-morrow the cord may be round thy neck, and thou be in need of breath; now lord, the cord for mine—"

Cathal smiled grimly.

"Blackheart," he said, "thou hast no lack of courage. Now up," and he loosened her hands, "and fly if thou wilt—swim the ditch, and get thee to Drumcoll-choille—and Guthbinn shall die in thy stead. What? Thou wouldst liefer die? Back then to yonder chamber, where my men will deal with thee as I have ordered, and be as patient as in thee lies. A kiss first, Red-Hair; and hearken from yonder chamber if thou wilt, while Aonan sings a dirge for thee."

She went; and presently there rang from within the chamber the shrill scream of a woman's agony, and Cathal laughed to see Aonan's face turn white. "She is not as patient as thou," he said, "but she will learn. Keep thou my word to her, Aonan: sing a dirge for her beauty a-dying."

"I cannot sing," Aonan-na-Righ said,

shivering as there rose another shriek. "Let them slay her, my lord, and have done."

"My will runs otherwise," said Cathal, smiling. "Sing, if thou lovest thy life."

"My lord knows that I do not," Aonan answered; and Cathal smiled again.

"Belike not; but sing and lessen the Dane's punishment. When the song is finished she shall be released, and even tended well."

So Aonan sang the song of the Dane-land over the water, and the Danes that died in the Valley of Keening — which is now called Waterford; of the white skin and red hair of Astrild; of her grace and daring; of the sons that lay dead on the battleplace; of Coloman the dreamer that read the stars; and of the beautiful boy whose breast was a nest of nightingales. And then he sang—more softly—of the Isle of the Noble where Acaill dwelt, and how she would have shadowed Astrild with her pity if she had lived; and then he stopped singing and knelt before the King, dumb for a moment with the passion of his pity, for from the open door they could hear a woman moaning still.

"Lord," he said, "make an end. My life for hers—if a life the king must have; or my pain for hers—if the King must need feed his ears with cries."

"Graciously spoken, and like Acaill's son," King Cathal said. "And Astrild shall be set free. You within the chamber take the Dane to her son the lord Coloman's keeping; and thou, my son Aonan, tarry here till I return. I may have a fancy to send thee with a message to thy mother before dawn. Nay, but come with me, and we will go see Coloman, and ask how his mother does. Give me thine arm to lean on; I am tired, I am old, and an end has come to my pleasure in slaying. . . . Coloman!"

They were in Coloman's chamber now, and the Druid turned from star-gazing to greet the King, with a new dark look in his gentle face. "Coloman, how does thy mother do now? She had grown too bold in her pride, but we did not slay her because of Aonan here. How works our medicine that we designed to temper her beauty?"

"Well, lord. No man will kiss my mother's beauty more."

"Good: now she will turn her feet into ways of gentleness, perhaps. Thou holdest me a grudge for this medicine o' mine, my son Coloman?"

"Lord, she is my mother," the Druid said, looking down.

"The scars will heal," Cathal said; but—

Aonan here has only seen her beautiful. Coloman, wouldst thou have him see her scarred and foul to see?"

"No, lord," the Druid said fiercely. Cathal laughed.

"Have a gift of me, then, O Coloman," he said. "Spare him from sight of a marred beauty, in what way thou canst. I give thee his eyes for thy mother's scars."

The two young men looked at each other steadily: then Aonan spoke. "Take the payment that the King offers thee, Coloman, without fear: a debt is a debt."

"And the debt is heavy."

Coloman said hoarsely: "Lord, wilt thou go and leave Aonan-na-Righ to me? And wilt thou send to me thy cunning men, Flathartach and Fadhar? I must have help."

"Aonan-na-Righ will not hinder thee, Coloman," said the King, mockingly. "He desires greatly to meet with his mother: and do thou commend me also to the Lady Eivir, whom I wedded first, and who loved me well."

"Call me also to thy mother's memory," Toran the boaster cried presently, when all was made ready, and Coloman bade draw the irons from the brazier—"if thou goest so far, Darling of the King."

"I will remember," Aonan said: and then fire and flesh met.

  * * * * *

At the next Beltane feast Cathal the Red slept beside Acaill in the burial-place of the kings at Brugh, and Guthbinn sat in the high seat, Toran the boaster at his right hand. But Coloman the Druid stood on the tower-top, reading the faces of the stars; and along the road that wound its dusty way to the country of the Golden Hostages there toiled two dark figures: a woman and a man. Now the woman was hooded and masked, but under the gray hood the moonlight found a gleam of ruddy hair; and the man she led by the hand and watched over as a mother watches her son. Yet the woman was Danish Astrild, and the blind man was Aonan-na-Righ.

Glossary.

GLOSSARY.

Brigit.

There were three famous women of this name, not akin to either St. Bridget or the Bridget who was goddess of wisdom. The third of the name was Brigit Ambui, who procured for Irish women a part of succession: *i.e.*, a third part of the estate if there were no sons to inherit.

Brighid.

This Brighid was goddess of wisdom among the Dé Dananns: she was daughter of Aongus the Young, Master of Love.

Clan Colla.

Hostages taken from this clan (descended from the three Collas, grandsons of King Cairbre Lifféchar, and famous in Ulster, Connaught, Meath, and Scotland) had a right to wear golden fetters, and were called Orgiallans or Golden Hostages. The King of the Clan Colla had also the right to sit next to the High King of Ireland.

Dagdé.

Head of the Dé Danann gods: Master of Wealth and giver of good fortune. He is Master of the Dead, too; and wears a grey cloak and rides a grey horse like Odin of the North.

Dark Joan.

A wandering fairy, who occasionally adopts the extraordinary disguise of a clutch of chickens.

Diarmuid O'Duibhne.

Or Dermot O'Dyna: one of the chief Fenian heroes. In ballads and legends he plays a very prominent part, with Grania, Fionn's wife, whom he loved and carried off from Fionn.

Dust Dancing.

When the dust dances or dead leaves whirl by, the Folk of Faerie are passing, and it is well to draw back from the road, and give them place.

Drum-coll-choille.

Old name for Dublin. It means "At the back of the hazel-wood."

Earrach (Arragh.)

Spring.

Flower of Sorrow.

Stitchwort.

Foghmhar (Fowar).
Autumn.

Geimhridh (Gevre).
Winter.

Gentle Colour.
Green. The word gentle is used in some parts of Ireland to signify things " elfin " or of fairy origin.

Geasa.
Bonds under which the heroes were frequently put. Thus: the fairy Niamh laid Oisin under geasa not to dismount from his fairy steed lest old age should come suddenly upon him: Dermot O'Dyna was under geasa not to hunt the boar.

Greenan.
The sunny chamber where the lady of the house spent the daylight hours, working among her women.

The Hounds.
These were devil-dogs which lay in wait for the passing soul, to catch and devour it on its way to the Judgment-seat. For three hours after death, therefore, the keeners refrained from wailing over the dead lest these ban-dogs should be awakened.

Half-Summer.
Wallflower.

Saint Idé.

She is the Bridget of Munster; and was the first to build a convent on Munster soil. Its site is called Killedy to this day, although the name of the Saint has almost passed from the memory of Limerick folk.

Kasár.

She was a queen, and afterwards a goddess, among the Fomoroh, or Fomorians, the forgotten giant race of hunters and fishers who wore through the dark time before the dawn of Irish history.

Kathaleen Ny-Houlahan.

One of the many mythical names of Ireland.

Kistvaen.

A rude stone coffin wherein either the unburnt body, or the urn full of ashes was disposed. The kistvaens were never buried very deeply, but were placed near the surface of the earth.

Leprechaun.

A little fairy cobbler, who sits clouting elfin shoes under hedges in the summer-time. Kept carefully in sight he will discover buried treasure to his persecutor: but he is wily and a tricksy spirit, and the treasure does not often pass into human hands.

Lug Lamfada.

The Irish Mercury: patron of arts and artificers. He was lord, too, of wit and cunning.

Lament of the Lay Brother.

'Where cattle are there are milkmaids, and woman is the root of all evil,' said St. Columba: and he refused to allow his monks to pasture their kine in the green meadows of Iona: a refusal which the lay brothers must have much lamented as they looked down on the empty meadows.

Lissakeole.

Certain haunted raths in the south of Ireland, where fairy music may sometimes yet be heard. Whoever chances to hear this "Ceol-Sidhe" loses all passion of hate and love, and cares for nothing but the music in his ears, and wastes to death with the desire and delight of it.

Manannan.

God of the seas around Ireland. The Isle of Man was one of his enchanted islands: and all the merrows (mermaids) in Irish waters owed allegiance to him.

Quicken.

This, the mountain ash, is one of the holiest trees of Irish tradition. It is sacred to the Gentle People, and in the Isle of the Blessed the happy dead dwell under " woven roofs of quicken boughs " as W. B. Yeats has exquisitely described in " A Man that Dreamed of Fairyland."

Ros geal dhu !

Another name of Ireland. Its literal meaning is (I think) the Beautiful Dark Rose.

Silk of the Kine.
Another metaphorical name for Ireland.

Samhradh (Sowra).
Summer.

Tympan.
A small stringed instrument, played like a violin.

Una of the West.
Una is queen over the Shee or Fairy-Folk of the western parts of Ireland : but she shares her sovereignty with a great many other fairy monarchs: Finarra, Cleena, Eerin, Donal Gealach, Macananty, Mab, and many others who rule a shadowy people from a shadowy throne.

Worlds Delight.
Dog-violet.

I WISH here to acknowledge the kindness of the Publisher of *The Yellow Book* in allowing me to reprint the "Lament of the Last Leprechaun" and "Aonan-na-Righ" from the October quarterly number: and also to thank the Proprietors of *Household Words* and *Sylvia's Journal* for their courtesy in permitting me to reproduce "Daluan" and "Boholaun and I," which appeared in their respective journals.

Printed by R. Folkard & Son,
22, Devonshire St., Queen Sq., London.

List of Books
IN
Belles Lettres

All the Books in this Catalogue
are Published at Net Prices

1894

Telegraphic Address
Bodleian, London

December, 1894.

List of Books
IN
BELLES LETTRES
(Including some Transfers)
Published by John Lane
𝕿𝖍𝖊 𝕭𝖔𝖉𝖑𝖊𝖞 𝕳𝖊𝖆𝖉
Vigo Street, London, W.

N.B.—The Authors and Publisher reserve the right of reprinting any book in this list if a new edition is called for, except in cases where a stipulation has been made to the contrary, and of printing a separate edition of any of the books for America irrespective of the numbers to which the English editions are limited. The numbers mentioned do not include copies sent to the public libraries. nor those sent for review. Most of the books are published simultaneously in England and America, and in many instances the names of the American publishers are appended.

ADAMS (FRANCIS).
    ESSAYS IN MODERNITY. Cr. 8vo. 5s. net. [*Shortly.*
    Chicago: Stone & Kimball.

ADAMS (FRANCIS).
    A CHILD OF THE AGE. Cr. 8vo. 3s. 6d. net.
      (See KEYNOTES SERIES.) [*Immediately.*
    Boston: Roberts Bros.

ALLEN (GRANT).
  THE LOWER SLOPES : A Volume of Verse. With title-page and cover design by J. ILLINGWORTH KAY. 600 copies. Cr. 8vo. 5s. net.
  Chicago: Stone & Kimball.

ALLEN (GRANT).
  THE WOMAN WHO DID. Cr. 8vo. 3s. 6d. net.
    (*See* KEYNOTES SERIES.) [*In rapid preparation.*
  Boston: Roberts Bros.

BEARDSLEY (AUBREY).
  THE STORY OF VENUS AND TANNHÄUSER, in which is set forth an exact account of the Manner of State held by Madam Venus, Goddess and Meretrix, under the famous Hörselberg, and containing the adventures of Tannhäuser in that place, his repentance, his journeying to Rome, and return to the loving Mountain. By AUBREY BEARDSLEY. With 20 full-page illustrations, numerous ornaments, and a cover from the same hand. Sq. 16mo. 10s. 6d. net. [*In preparation.*

BEECHING (Rev. H. C.).
  IN A GARDEN: Poems. With a specially-designed title-page. Cr. 8vo. 5s. net. [*In preparation.*

BENSON (ARTHUR CHRISTOPHER).
  LYRICS. Fcap. 8vo. 5s. net. [*In rapid preparation.*

BROTHERTON (MARY).
  ROSEMARY FOR REMEMBRANCE. With title-page designed by WALTER WEST. Fcap. 8vo. 5s. net.
    [*In rapid preparation.*

DALMON (C. W.).
  SONG FAVOURS. With a specially-designed title-page. Sq. 16mo. 4s. 6d. net. [*In preparation.*

D'ARCY (ELLA).
  A VOLUME OF STORIES. Cr. 8vo. 3s. 6d. net.
    [*In preparation.*
    (*See* KEYNOTES SERIES.)
  Boston: Roberts Bros.

DAVIDSON (JOHN).
    PLAYS: An Unhistorical Pastoral; A Romantic Farce Bruce, a Chronicle Play; Smith, a Tragic Farce; Scaramouch in Naxos, a Pantomime. With a frontispiece and cover design by AUBREY BEARDSLEY. Printed at the Ballantyne Press. 500 copies. Sm. 4to. 7s. 6d. net.
    Chicago: Stone & Kimball.

DAVIDSON (JOHN).
    FLEET ST. ECLOGUES. 2nd edition. Fcap. 8vo., buckram. 5s. net.

DAVIDSON (JOHN).
    A RANDOM ITINERARY AND A BALLAD. With a frontispiece and title-page by LAURENCE HOUSMAN. 600 copies. Fcap. 8vo., Irish linen. 5s. net.
    Boston: Copeland & Day.

DAVIDSON (JOHN).
    THE NORTH WALL. Fcap. 8vo. 2s. 6d. net.
    The few remaining copies transferred by the Author to the present Publisher.

DAVIDSON (JOHN).
    BALLADS AND SONGS. With title-page designed by WALTER WEST. Fcap. 8vo., buckram. 5s. net.
    Boston: Copeland & Day.

DE TABLEY (LORD).
    POEMS, DRAMATIC AND LYRICAL. By JOHN LEICESTER WARREN (Lord De Tabley). Illustrations and cover design by C. S. RICKETTS. 2nd edition. Cr. 8vo. 7s. 6d. net.

DE TABLEY (LORD).
    NEW POEMS. Cr. 8vo. 5s. net.   [*In preparation.*

EGERTON (GEORGE).
    KEYNOTES. 6th edition. Cr. 8vo. 3s. 6d. net.
    (*See* KEYNOTES SERIES.)
    Boston: Roberts Bros.

EGERTON (GEORGE).
  DISCORDS. Cr. 8vo. 3s. 6d. net.
  (See KEYNOTES SERIES.) [*In rapid preparation.*
  Boston: Roberts Bros.

EGERTON (GEORGE).
  YOUNG OFEG'S DITTIES. A translation from the Swedish of OLA HANSSON. Cr. 8vo. 3s. 6d. net.
  [*In preparation.*

FARR (FLORENCE).
  THE DANCING FAUN. Cr. 8vo. 3s. 6d. net.
  (See KEYNOTES SERIES.)
  Boston: Roberts Bros.

FLETCHER (J. S.).
  THE WONDERFUL WAPENTAKE. By "A SON OF THE SOIL." With 18 full-page illustrations on Japanese vellum, by J. A. SYMINGTON. Cr. 8vo. 5s. 6d. net.
  [*In rapid preparation.*

GALE (NORMAN).
  ORCHARD SONGS, with title-page and cover design by J. ILLINGWORTH KAY. Fcap. 8vo., Irish linen. 5s. net.
  Also a special edition, limited in number, on hand-made paper, bound in English vellum. £1. 1s. net.
  New York: G. P. Putnam's Sons.

GARNETT (RICHARD).
  POEMS. With title-page by J. ILLINGWORTH KAY. 350 copies. Cr. 8vo. 5s. net.
  Boston: Copeland & Day.

GOSSE (EDMUND).
  THE LETTERS OF THOMAS LOVELL BEDDOES. Now first edited. Pott 8vo. 5s. net.
  New York: Macmillan & Co.

GRAHAME (KENNETH).
  PAGAN PAPERS: A VOLUME OF ESSAYS. With title-page by AUBREY BEARDSLEY. Fcap. 8vo. 5s. net.
  Chicago: Stone & Kimball.

GREENE (G. A.).
 ITALIAN LYRISTS OF TO-DAY. Translations in the original metres from about 35 living Italian poets ; with bibliographical and biographical notes. Cr. 8vo. 5s. net.
 New York: Macmillan & Co.

GREENWOOD (FREDERICK).
 IMAGINATION IN DREAMS. Cr. 8vo. 5s. net.
 [*In rapid preparation.*]

HAKE (T. GORDON).
 A SELECTION FROM HIS POEMS. Edited by Mrs. MEYNELL, with a portrait after D. G. ROSSETTI, and a cover design by GLEESON WHITE. Cr. 8vo. 5s. net.
 Chicago: Stone & Kimball.

HARLAND (HENRY).
 THE BOHEMIAN GIRL, AND OTHER STORIES. Cr. 8vo. 3s. 6d. net. (*See* KEYNOTES SERIES). [*In preparation.*]
 Boston: Roberts Bros.

HAYES (ALFRED).
 THE VALE OF ARDEN, AND OTHER POEMS. With a title-page designed by E. H. NEW. Fcap. 8vo. 3s. 6d. net.
 [*In preparation.*]

HEINEMANN (WILLIAM).
 THE FIRST STEP: A Dramatic Moment. Sm. 4to. 3s. 6d. net.
 [*Immediately.*]

HOPPER (NORA).
 BALLADS IN PROSE. With a title-page and cover by WALTER WEST. Sq. 16mo. 5s. net.
 Boston: Roberts Bros.

IRVING (LAURENCE).
 GODEFROI AND YOLANDE: A Play. With 3 illustrations by AUBREY BEARDSLEY. Sm. 4to. 5s. net.
 [*In preparation.*]

JAMES (W. P.).
 ROMANTIC PROFESSIONS: A volume of Essays. With title-page designed by J. ILLINGWORTH KAY. Cr. 8vo. 5s. net.
 New York: Macmillan & Co.

JOHNSON (LIONEL).
   THE ART OF THOMAS HARDY. Six Essays, with etched portrait by WM. STRANG, and Bibliography by JOHN LANE. Cr. 8vo. Buckram. 5s. 6d. net.
   Also 150 copies, large paper, with proofs of the portrait. £1. 1s. net. [*Just published.*
   New York: Dodd, Mead & Co

JOHNSON (PAULINE).
   WHITE WAMPUM : Poems. Cr. 8vo. 5s. net.
   [*In preparation.*

JOHNSTONE (C. E.).
   BALLADS OF BOY AND BEAK. Fcap. 8vo. 2s. 6d. net.
   [*In preparation.*

KEYNOTES SERIES.
   Each volume with specially-designed title-page by AUBREY BEARDSLEY. Cr. 8vo. cloth. 3s. 6d. net.
   Vol. I. KEYNOTES. By GEORGE EGERTON.
   [*Sixth Edition now ready.*
   Vol. II. THE DANCING FAUN. By FLORENCE FARR.
   Vol. III. POOR FOLK. Translated from the Russian of F. DOSTOIEVSKY by LENA MILMAN, with a preface by GEORGE MOORE.
   Vol. IV. A CHILD OF THE AGE. By FRANCIS ADAMS.
   Vol. V. THE GREAT GOD PAN AND THE INMOST LIGHT. By ARTHUR MACHEN.
   [*About December 1st.*
   Vol. VI. DISCORDS. By GEORGE EGERTON.
   [*About December 1st.*
   The following are in rapid preparation :—
   Vol. VII. PRINCE ZALESKI. By M. P. SHIEL.
   Vol. VIII. THE WOMAN WHO DID. By GRANT ALLEN.
   Vol. IX. WOMEN'S TRAGEDIES. By H. D. LOWRY.
   Vol. X. THE BOHEMIAN GIRL AND OTHER STORIES. By HENRY HARLAND.
   Vol. XI. A VOLUME OF STORIES. By H. B. MARRIOTT WATSON.
   Vol. XII. A VOLUME OF STORIES. By ELLA D'ARCY.
   Boston: Roberts Bros.

LEATHER (R. K.).
  VERSES. 250 copies, fcap. 8vo. 3s. net.
  Transferred by the Author to the present Publisher.

LE GALLIENNE (RICHARD).
  PROSE FANCIES, with a portrait of the Author, by WILSON STEER. Third edition. Cr. 8vo., purple cloth, uniform with "The Religion of a Literary Man." 5s. net.
  Also a limited large paper edition. 12s. 6d. net.
  New York: G. P. Putnam's Sons.

LE GALLIENNE (RICHARD).
  THE BOOK BILLS OF NARCISSUS. An account rendered by RICHARD LE GALLIENNE Third edition, cr. 8vo., purple cloth, uniform with "The Religion of a Literary Man." 3s. 6d. net. [*In rapid preparation.*

LE GALLIENNE (RICHARD).
  ENGLISH POEMS. Third edition, cr. 8vo. purple cloth, uniform with "The Religion of a Literary Man." 5s net.
  Boston: Copeland & Day.

LE GALLIENNE (RICHARD).
  GEORGE MEREDITH: Some Characteristics; with a Bibliography (much enlarged) by JOHN LANE, portrait, &c. Fourth edition, cr 8vo., purple cloth, uniform with "The Religion of a Literary Man." 5s. 6d. net.

LE GALLIENNE (RICHARD).
  THE RELIGION OF A LITERARY MAN. 5th thousand. Cr. 8vo., purple cloth. 3s. 6d. net.
  Also a special rubricated edition on hand-made paper. 8vo. 10s. 6d. net.
  New York: G. P. Putnam's Sons.

LOWRY (H. D.).
  WOMEN'S TRAGEDIES. Cr. 8vo. 3s. 6d. net.
    (*See* KEYNOTES SERIES.) [*In preparation.*
  Boston: Roberts Bros.

LUCAS (WINIFRED).
    A Volume of Poems. Fcap. 8vo. 4s. 6d. net.
                                                               [*In preparation.*

MACHEN (ARTHUR).
    The Great God Pan and The Inmost Light. Cr. 8vo. 3s. 6d. net.
    (*See* Keynotes Series.)   [*In rapid preparation.*
    Boston: Roberts Bros.

MARZIALS (THEO.).
    The Gallery of Pigeons, and Other Poems. Post 8vo. 4s. 6d. net.   [*Very few remain.*
    Transferred by the Author to the present Publisher.

MEREDITH (GEORGE).
    The First Published Portrait of this Author, engraved on the wood by W. Biscombe Gardner, after the painting by G. F. Watts. Proof copies on Japanese vellum, signed by painter and engraver. £1. 1s. net.

MEYNELL (MRS.) (ALICE C. THOMPSON).
    Poems. 2nd edition. Fcap. 8vo. 3s. 6d. net. A few of the 50 large paper copies (1st edition) remain. 12s. 6d. net.

MEYNELL (MRS.).
    The Rhythm of Life, and Other Essays. 2nd edition. Fcap. 8vo. 3s. 6d. net. A few of the 50 large paper copies (1st edition) remain. 12s. 6d. net.

MILLER (JOAQUIN).
    The Building of the City Beautiful. Fcap. 8vo. With a decorated cover. 5s. net.   [*Just published.*
    Chicago: Stone & Kimball.

MILMAN (LENA).
    Poor Folk. Translated from the Russian of F. Dostoievsky. (*See* Keynotes Series.) Cr. 8vo. 3s. 6d. net.
    Boston: Roberts Bros.

MONKHOUSE (ALLAN).
BOOKS AND PLAYS: A VOLUME OF ESSAYS ON MEREDITH, BORROW, IBSEN, AND OTHERS. 400 copies. Cr. 8vo. 5s. net.
Philadelphia: J. B. Lippincott Co.

NESBIT (E.).
A VOLUME OF POEMS. Cr. 8vo. 5s. net.
[*In preparation.*

NETTLESHIP (J. T.).
ROBERT BROWNING. Essays and Thoughts. 3rd edition, with a portrait. Cr. 8vo. 5s. 6d. net.
[*In rapid preparation.*
New York: Chas. Scribner's Sons.

NOBLE (JAS. ASHCROFT).
THE SONNET IN ENGLAND. AND OTHER ESSAYS. Title-page and cover design by AUSTIN YOUNG. 600 copies. Cr. 8vo. 5s. net. Also 50 copies L.P. 12s. 6d. net.

O'SHAUGHNESSY (ARTHUR).
HIS LIFE AND HIS WORK. With selections from his Poems. By LOUISE CHANDLER MOULTON. Portrait and cover design. Fcap. 8vo. 5s. net.
[*Just published.*
Chicago: Stone & Kimball.

OXFORD CHARACTERS.
A series of lithographed Portraits by WILL ROTHENSTEIN, with text by F. YORK POWELL and others. To be issued monthly in term. Each number will contain two portraits. Parts I. to V. ready. 200 sets only, folio, wrapper, 5s. net per part: 25 special large paper sets containing proof impressions of the portraits signed by the artist, 10s. 6d. net per part.

PETERS (WM. THEODORE).
POSIES OUT OF RINGS. Sq. 16mo. 3s. 6d. net.
[*In preparation.*

PLARR (VICTOR).
    A VOLUME OF POEMS. Cr. 8vo. 5s. net.
                                        [*In preparation.*

RICKETTS (C. S.) AND C. H. SHANNON.
    HERO AND LEANDER. By CHRISTOPHER MARLOWE and GEORGE CHAPMAN. With borders, initials, and illustrations designed and engraved on the wood by C. S. RICKETTS and C. H. SHANNON. Bound in English vellum and gold 200 copies only. 35s. net.
    Boston: Copeland & Day.

RHYS (ERNEST).
    A LONDON ROSE AND OTHER RHYMES. With title-page designed by SELWYN IMAGE. 350 copies. Cr. 8vo. 5s. net.
    New York: Dodd, Mead, & Co.

SHIEL (M. P.).
    PRINCE ZALESKI. Cr 8vo. 3s. 6d. net.
        (*See* KEYNOTES SERIES.)   [*In preparation.*
    Boston: Roberts Bros.

STREET (G. S.).
    THE AUTOBIOGRAPHY OF A BOY. Passages selected by his friend, G. S. S. With title-page designed by C. W. FURSE. Fcap. 8vo. 3s. 6d. net.
                                [*Fourth Edition now ready.*
    Philadelphia: J. B. Lippincott Co.

SYMONS (ARTHUR).
    A NEW VOLUME OF POEMS. Cr. 8vo. 5s. net.
                                        [*In preparation.*

THOMPSON (FRANCIS).
    A VOLUME OF POEMS. With frontispiece, title-page, and cover design by LAURENCE HOUSMAN. 4th edition. Pott 4to. 5s. net.
    Boston: Copeland & Day.

TREE (H BEERBOHM).
    THE IMAGINATIVE FACULTY: a Lecture delivered at the Royal Institution. With portrait of Mr. TREE from an unpublished drawing by the Marchioness of Granby. Fcap. 8vo., boards. 2s. 6d. net.

TYNAN HINKSON (KATHARINE).
    CUCKOO SONGS. With title-page and cover design by LAURENCE HOUSMAN. Fcap. 8vo. 5s. net.
    Boston: Copeland & Day.

TYNAN HINKSON (KATHARINE).
    MIRACLE PLAYS. [*In preparation.*

WATSON (H. B. MARRIOTT).
    A VOLUME OF STORIES. Cr. 8vo. 3s. 6d. net.
    (*See* KEYNOTES SERIES.) [*In preparation.*
    Boston: Roberts Bros.

WATSON (WILLIAM).
    ODES, AND OTHER POEMS. Fcap. 8vo. 4s. 6d. net.
    [*About December* 1st.
    New York: Macmillan & Co.

WATSON (WILLIAM).
    THE ELOPING ANGELS: A CAPRICE. 2nd edition. Sq. 16mo, buckram. 3s. 6d. net.
    New York: Macmillan & Co.

WATSON (WILLIAM).
    EXCURSIONS IN CRITICISM: BEING SOME PROSE RECREATIONS OF A RHYMER. 2nd edition, cr. 8vo. 5s. net.
    New York: Macmillan & Co.

WATSON (WILLIAM).
    THE PRINCE'S QUEST, AND OTHER POEMS. With a bibliographical note added. 2nd edition, fcap. 8vo. 4s. 6d. net.

WATTS (THEODORE).
    POEMS. Cr. 8vo. 5s. net. [*In preparation.*
    There will also be an Edition de Luxe *of this volume printed at the Kelmscott Press.*

WHARTON (H. T.).
    SAPPHO Memoir, text, selected renderings, and a literal translation by HENRY THORNTON WHARTON. With three illustrations, fcap. 8vo. 7s. 6d. net.
                                          [*In preparation.*

WILDE (OSCAR).
    THE SPHINX. A Poem. Decorated throughout in line and colour and bound in a design by CHARLES RICKETTS. 250 copies, £2. 2s. net. 25 copies large paper, £5. 5s. net.
    Boston: Copeland & Day.

WILDE (OSCAR).
    The incomparable and ingenious history of Mr. W. H., being the true secret of Shakespear's sonnets, now for the first time here fully set forth. With initial letters and cover design by CHARLES RICKETTS. 500 copies, 10s. 6d. net. Also 50 copies large paper, 21s. net.
                                          [*In preparation.*

WILDE (OSCAR).
    DRAMATIC WORKS, now printed for the first time. With a specially-designed binding to each volume, by CHARLES SHANNON. 500 copies, sm. 4to., 7s. 6d. net per vol. Also 50 copies large paper, 15s. net per vol.
        Vol. I. LADY WINDERMERE'S FAN. A comedy in four acts. [*Out of print.*
        Vol. II. A WOMAN OF NO IMPORTANCE. A comedy in four acts. [*Just published.*
        Vol. III. THE DUCHESS OF PADUA. A blank verse tragedy in five acts. [*Very shortly.*
    Boston: Copeland & Day.

WILDE (OSCAR).
    SALOME. A Tragedy in one act, done into English, with 10 illustrations, title-page, tail-piece, and cover design by AUBREY BEARDSLEY. 500 copies, sm. 4to. 15s. net. Also 100 copies large paper, 30s. net.
    Boston: Copeland & Day.

The Yellow Book.
An Illustrated Quarterly.

VOL. I. Fourth Edition, pott 4to., 272 pp., 15 Illustrations, Decorative Cloth Cover, price 5s. net.

The Letterpress by MAX BEERBOHM, A. C. BENSON, HUBERT CRACKANTHORPE, ELLA D'ARCY, JOHN DAVIDSON, GEORGE EGERTON, RICHARD GARNETT, EDMUND GOSSE, HENRY HARLAND, JOHN OLIVER HOBBES, HENRY JAMES, RICHARD LE GALLIENNE, GEORGE MOORE, GEORGE SAINTSBURY, FRED M. SIMPSON, ARTHUR SYMONS, WILLIAM WATSON, ARTHUR WAUGH.

The Illustrations by SIR FREDERIC LEIGHTON, P.R.A., AUBREY BEARDSLEY, R. ANNING BELL, CHARLES W. FURSE, LAURENCE HOUSMAN, J. T. NETTLESHIP, JOSEPH PENNELL, WILL ROTHENSTEIN, WALTER SICKERT.

VOL. II. Third Edition, pott 4to., 364 pp., 23 Illustrations, with a New Decorative Cloth Cover, price 5s. net.

The Literary Contributions by FREDERICK GREENWOOD, ELLA D'ARCY, CHARLES WILLEBY, JOHN DAVIDSON, HENRY HARLAND, DOLLIE RADFORD, CHARLOTTE M. MEW, AUSTIN DOBSON, V., O., C. S., KATHARINE DE MATTOS, PHILIP GILBERT HAMERTON, RONALD CAMPBELL MACFIE, DAUPHIN MEUNIER, KENNETH GRAHAME, NORMAN GALE, NETTA SYRETT, HUBERT CRACKANTHORPE, ALFRED HAYES, MAX BEERBOHM, WILLIAM WATSON, and HENRY JAMES.

The Art Contributions by WALTER CRANE, A S. HARTRICK, AUBREY BEARDSLEY, ALFRED THORNTON, P. WILSON STEER, JOHN S. SARGENT, A.R.A., SYDNEY ADAMSON, WALTER SICKERT, W. BROWN MACDOUGAL, E. J. SULLIVAN, FRANCIS FORSTER, BERNHARD SICKERT, and AYMER VALLANCE.

A Special Feature of Volume II. is a frank criticism of the Literature and Art of Volume I. by PHILIP GILBERT HAMERTON.

The Yellow Book.

VOL. III. Now ready, pott 4to., 280 pp., 15 Illustrations, with a New Decorative Cloth Cover, price 5s. net.

The Literary Contributions by WILLIAM WATSON, KENNETH GRAHAME, ARTHUR SYMONS, ELLA D'ARCY, JOSÉ MARIA DE HÉRÉDIA, ELLEN M. CLERKE, HENRY HARLAND, THEO. MARZIALS, ERNEST DOWSON, THEODORE WRATISLAW, ARTHUR MOORE, OLIVE CUSTANCE, LIONEL JOHNSON, ANNIE MACDONELL, C. S., NORA HOPPER, S. CORNISH WATKINS, HUBERT CRACKANTHORPE, MORTON FULLERTON, LEILA MACDONALD, C. W. DALMON, MAX BEERBOHM, and JOHN DAVIDSON.

The Art Contributions by PHILIP BROUGHTON, GEORGE THOMSON, AUBREY BEARDLEY, ALBERT FOSCITER, WALTER SICKERT, P. WILSON STEER, WILLIAM HYDE, and MAX BEERBOHM.

Prospectuses Post Free on Application.

Boston : *Copeland & Day.*

www.ingramcontent.com/pod-product-compliance
Lightning Source LLC
Chambersburg PA
CBHW020913230426
43666CB00008B/1441